TEACH YOURSELF BOOKS

W9-BZX-754

MODERN GREEK

A good introduction to Modern Greek, clearly set out. A complete grammar of the language is provided, together with exercises. At the end of the book will be found both a Greek–English and an English–Greek vocabulary. Mr. Julian Pring has provided an invaluable phonetic introduction.

The Times Literary Supplement

TEACH YOURSELF BOOKS

MODERN GREEK

S. A. Sofroniou, M.A., Ph.D., M.Sc.

with a Phonetic Introduction by

J. T. Pring, M.A.

Long-renowned as *the* authoritative source for self-guided learning – with more than 30 million copies sold worldwide – the *Teach Yourself* series includes over 200 titles in the fields of languages, crafts, hobbies, sports, and other leisure activities.

This edition was first published in 1993 by NTC Publishing Group, 4255 West Touhy Avenue, Lincolnwood (Chicago), Illinois 60646 – 1975 U.S.A. Originally published by Hodder and Stoughton Ltd.
Copyright 1962 by S. A. Sofroniou
All rights reserved. No part of this book may be reproduced, stored in a retrieval system, or transmitted in any form, or by any means, electronic, mechanical, photocopying, or otherwise, without prior permission of NTC Publishing Group.

Library of Congress Catalog Card Number: 92–82506

Printed and bound in Great Britain by
Cox & Wyman Ltd, Reading, Berkshire

CONTENTS

CONTENTS

CONTENTS

PART II: INVARIABLE WORDS.

CONTENTS

INTRODUCTION

The Modern Greek language is spoken by about ten million people inhabiting mainly two states, Greece and Cyprus.

It constitutes the present stage in the natural development of the language from classical Greek through *koine* or New Testament Greek and Byzantine or Medieval Greek to the present day. Like all languages it has undergone various changes in both pronunciation, grammar and vocabulary throughout its long historical course.

The idiom of present-day Athens has been used as the model of the modern language which is described in this book. It must be borne in mind, however, that some people use dialectal forms (especially in Cyprus, Crete and Northern Greece) as well as forms belonging to previous stages in the development of the language. The latter forms constitute the so-called *katharevousa* language which is used mainly in the writing of official documents, some school-books and partly in newspapers.

The grammar of any language is like the map of a country. It attempts to portray all the main features of a territory but it cannot describe it completely. That is why exceptions are such a common and necessary part of any grammar. The main features of Modern Greek outlined in this book have been statistically determined from samples of both present-day Athenian speech and writing contained mainly in novels dealing with contemporary Athenian life.

The amount of space devoted to different forms, and the order in which they are dealt with has also been mainly determined by their relative frequency of occurrence. It is hoped that this will benefit the student by directing his attention and effort to the fundamental elements of the language.

It is a pleasant duty to thank Mr. Julian Pring not only for his Phonetic Introduction but also for his constant and fruitful guidance, criticism and help throughout the writing of this book; Dr. David Phillips has also kindly put at my disposal his great knowledge of both demotic Greek and linguistics.

S. A. Sofroniou

PHONETIC INTRODUCTION

Modern Greek is written with the same alphabet as ancient Greek, and the main body of vocabulary has been handed down from classical times with its spelling virtually unchanged. Naturally the pronunciation has altered in the course of time. But nobody can know what classical Greek sounded like, and there is no reason to suppose that the language sounded any "better" then than it does today.

Students of Greek must learn to read and write the alphabet as quickly as possible. This is by no means difficult for English speakers. Almost all the sounds are easy to make; and when once you have learnt the phonetic values of the letters, you can read the written language automatically, because the spelling is logical and always preserves those same values.

In order to give you a starting-point, the Greek orthography in this chapter is accompanied by a simple transcription into Roman letters; and the sounds are described in detail, with reference to their nearest English equivalents. The letters of this transcription are always enclosed within square brackets. Of course, this method cannot tell you accurately enough what the quality of the sounds is like. It is very important for you to listen to the speech of a native Greek as soon as you can, so that you may check and amplify what you have read in the book by what you hear in real life. In the long run you can only acquire a Greek accent by imitating Greeks.

Pay careful attention to the exercises in this chapter, because from here onwards only the Greek spelling will be given, and you will not have a phonetic transcription to help you.

THE SOUNDS OF GREEK

Vowels

[a] similar to *o* in *love.*
[e] „ „ *e* in *sell.*
[i] „ „ *i* in *police.*
[o] „ „ *o* in *got.*
[u] „ „ *oo* in *root.*

Consonants

[b d f g k m n p t v z] as in English.
[dh] similar to *th* in *this.*
[gh] „ „ *g* in Spanish *Aragon* (phonetic symbol ɣ).
[kh] „ „ *ch* in German *ich* or *buch* (phonetic symbols ç, x).
[l] „ „ *l* in *least* (not *l* in *tall*).
[r] lightly rolled, as in Italian or Scottish.
[s] similar to *s* in *sit* (not *s* in *was*).
[th] „ „ *th* in *thick.*
[y] „ „ *y* in *you.*

Note (1): [p t k] should not be given the aspiration, or slight puff of breath before a vowel, which is usual in English.

Note (2): [n] before [k], [kh] and [g] has the same quality as in *ankle, angle,* etc.

Note (3): [kh] is also the sound of *ch* in Scottish *loch.* [gh] bears the same relation to [kh] as [g] does to [k].

ACCENT AND QUALITY

Every word bears a stress-accent on one of its syllables. In this transcription, the vowel of each stressed syllable is printed in italic. *Do not lengthen the stressed vowel as much as you would in English.* All Greek vowels, whether stressed or not, are relatively short, and preserve more or less the same quality in all positions. *Do not weaken unstressed vowels as you would in English.* In Greek every word is uttered precisely and swiftly, giving each syllable its full value without drawling or dawdling over it. Say the word [mar*i*a] (*Mary*). The first and third vowels must not be weakened as in English *Maria*. Nor is the [i] lengthened. In [monot*o*nos] (*monotonous*) each [o] has the same quality, although only one is stressed. Practise the following: [sin*o*nimos] (*synonymous*); [paralitik*o*s] (*paralytic*); [katastrof*i*] (*catastrophe*); [fil*o*sofos] (*philosopher*); [politik*o*s] (*political*); [an*a*lisis] (*analysis*); [ikonom*i*a] (*economy*); [ep*i*skopos] (*bishop*); [ip*o*thesis] (*hypothesis*); [therm*o*metron] (*thermometer*).

Pay special attention to final [e] and [o]. The word [ne] (*yes*) must not sound like English *nay*, but like *ne* in *never*. The second syllable of [vun*o*] (*mountain*) must not sound like English *know*, but like *kno* in *knot*.

THE GREEK ALPHABET

Α	*α*	*ἄλφα*	[*a*lfa]
Β	*β*	*βῆτα*	[v*i*ta]
Γ	*γ*	*γάμμα*	[gh*a*ma]
Δ	*δ*	*δέλτα*	[dh*e*lta]
Ε	*ε*	*ἔψιλον*	[*e*psilon]
Ζ	*ζ*	*ζῆτα*	[z*i*ta]
Η	*η*	*ἦτα*	[*i*ta]
Θ	*θ*	*θῆτα*	[th*i*ta]
Ι	*ι*	*ἰῶτα*	[i*o*ta]
Κ	*κ*	*κάππα*	[k*a*pa]
Λ	*λ*	*λάμ(β)δα*	[l*a*mdha]

Μ	*μ*	*μῦ*	[mi]
Ν	*ν*	*νῦ*	[ni]
Ξ	*ξ*	*ξῖ*	[ksi]
Ο	*ο*	*ὄμικρον*	[*o*mikron]
Π	*π*	*πῖ*	[pi]
Ρ	*ρ*	*ρῶ*	[ro]
Σ	*σ ς**	*σῖγμα*	[s*i*ghma]
Τ	*τ*	*ταῦ*	[taf]
Υ	*υ*	*ὔψιλον*	[*i*psilon]
Φ	*φ*	*φῖ*	[fi]
Χ	*χ*	*χῖ*	[khi]
Ψ	*ψ*	*ψῖ*	[psi]
Ω	*ω*	*ὠμέγα*	[om*e*gha]

* Used only at the end of a word.

PRONUNCIATION OF THE ALPHABET

α [a] *ἄρωμα* [*a*roma] *scent.*

β [v] *βίβλος* [v*i*vlos] *Bible.*

γ [gh] before *α*, *ο*, *ω*, *ου* and consonants: *γάτα* [gh*a*ta] *cat.*

[y] before *ε*, *αι*, *η*, *ι*, *υ*, *ει*, *οι*: *γένος* [y*e*nos] *genus.*

δ [dh] *δράμα* [dhr*a*ma] *drama.*

ε [e] *ἔρως* [*e*ros] *love.*

ζ [z] *ζῆλος* [z*i*los] *zeal.*

η [i] *ἡδονή* [idhon*i*] *pleasure.*

θ [th] *θέατρο* [th*e*atro] *theatre.*

ι [i] *ἰδέα* [idh*e*a] *idea.*

κ [k] *κεφάλι* [kef*a*li] *head.*

λ [l] *λίθος* [l*i*thos] *stone.*

μ [m] *μικρός* [mikr*o*s] *little.*

ν [n] *νέος* [n*e*os] *new, young.*

[ks] *ξύλο* [ks*i*lo] *wood.*

ο [o] *ὀκτώ* [okto] *eight.*
π [p] *πολύ* [poli] *much.*
ρ [r] *ρόλος* [rolos] *role.*
σ [z] before *β, γ, δ, ζ, (λ), μ, ν, ρ*: *κόσμος* [kozmos] *world.*
[s] elsewhere: *σειρά* [sira] *series.*
τ [t] *τραγωδία* [traghodhia] *tragedy.*
υ [i] *ὕπνος* [ipnos] *sleep.*
φ [f] *φάρμακο* [farmako] *medicine.*
χ [kh] before *α, ο, ω, ου* and consonants: *χορός* [khoros] *chorus, dance.*
As in German *ich* before *ε, αι, η, ι, υ, ει, οι*: *χημεία* [khimia] *chemistry.*
ψ [ps] *ψυχή* [psikhi] *soul.*
ω [o] *ὥρα* [ora] *hour.*

Apart from the above, certain groups of letters have special values:

αι [e] *αἰσθητικός* [esthitikos] *aesthetic.*
ει [i] *εἰρωνία* [ironia] *irony.*
οι [i] *οἰκονομία* [ikonomia] *economy.*
ου [u] *οὐτοπία* [utopia] *utopia.*
αυ [af] before *θ, κ, ξ, π, σ, τ, φ, χ, ψ*: *αὐτόματος* [aftomatos] *automatic.*
[av] elsewhere: *Αὔγουστος* [avghustos] *August.*
ευ [ef] before *θ, κ, ξ, π, σ, τ, φ, χ, ψ*: *εὐκάλυπτος* [efkaliptos] *eucalyptus.*
[ev] elsewhere: *Εὐρώπη* [evropi] *Europe.*
γγ [ng] *'Αγγλία* [anglia] *England.*
γκ [g] when initial: *γκαμήλα* [gamila] *camel.*
[ng] when medial: *ἄγκυρα* [angira] *anchor.*
γξ [nks] *φάλαγξ* [falanks] *phalanx.*
γχ [nkh] *μελαγχολία* [melankholia] *melancholy.*

μπ [b] when initial: *μπύρα* [b*i*ra] *beer.*
[mb] when medial: *Ὄλυμπος* [*o*limbos] *Olympus.*
ντ [d] when initial: *ντομάτα* [dom*a*ta] *tomato.*
[nd] when medial: *κέντρο* [k*e*ndro] *centre.*
τζ [dz] *τζάκι* [dz*a*ki] *hearth.*

Note. The pronunciation of *γκ*, *μπ*, *ντ* in the middle of a word may vary according to the particular word, and from one speaker to another. Thus the nasal element is sometimes omitted, leaving simply [g, b, d]. More rarely they are pronounced as [nk, mp, nt]. You can only learn these variations by experience.

With extremely few exceptions, a doubled consonant letter (apart from *γγ*) is pronounced as if it were single. Thus *Ἄννα Anne* is [*a*na], not [*a*nna] as in Italian.

DIACRITIC MARKS

Almost every word (unless written in capitals) has an accent over the vowel of its stressed syllable. There are three accents: *ὰ*, *ά*, *ᾶ*. You can ignore the difference between them; only their position is important.

An initial vowel, and sometimes initial *ρ*, bears one of two "breathings": *ἁ*, *ἀ*. These signs can be ignored.

The diaeresis is used to separate two letters which would otherwise have formed a group. Compare *καιρός* [ker*o*s] *weather*, and *Κάϊρο* [k*a*iro] *Cairo* (see p. 15).

PUNCTUATION

The comma and full stop are as in English. A raised dot (·) is the colon, and (;) is the question mark.

TRANSLITERATION

The connection between Greek words and their English derivatives is often very close, in form as well as in meaning. It may help you to bear in mind the usual way in which the Greek letters are transliterated in our own spelling. The following list gives some of the usual equivalents.

Greek letter	*Usual English equivalent*
η	e
υ	y
ω	o
αι	ae, e
ει	i, e
οι	oe, e
ου	u
β	b
γ	g
γκ, γγ	ng
κ	c
ρ-	rh-
φ	ph
χ	ch
(ʽ)	h-

Study the relation of spelling in these examples:

χορός	chorus	σχολεῖο	school
πολύ	(poly-)	εἴδωλον	idol
βίος	(bio-)	αἰσθητικός	aesthetic
ὕπνος	(hypnotic)	Κύπρος	Cyprus
μῦθος	myth	ρυθμός	rhythm
βίβλος	Bible	ὑγιεινός	hygienic

PHRASING

In ordinary speech, words are grouped together in short phrases. These are, phonetically, single units, and should be said as if they formed one word. Examples of such units are: article with noun, noun with possessive pronoun, negative particle with verb, etc. When we speak English the stress-accent falls mainly on *content-words* (nouns, verbs, adjectives, etc.) rather than on *form-words* (articles, conjunctions, prepositions, etc.). The same applies to Greek, where form-words are usually treated as unemphatic, even when they bear a written accent.

Practise the following:

Mary is at home.
ἡ Μαρία εἶναι στό σπίτι.
[imar*i*a *i*ne stosp*i*ti.]

didn't you see her hat?
δέν εἶδες τό καπέλλο της;
[dhen*i*dhes tokap*e*lotis?]

will you go on foot?
θά πᾶτε μέ τά πόδια;
[thap*a*te metap*o*dhia?]

please give it to me.
σέ παρακαλῶ νά μοῦ τό δόσεις.
[separakal*o* namutodh*o*sis.]

I like bathing by moonlight.
μοῦ ἀρέσει νά κολυμπῶ μέ τό φεγγάρι.
[muar*e*si nakolimb*o* metofeng*a*ri.]

Certain assimilations of sound may occur between adjacent words within a group:

Final ς is pronounced [z] if the next word begins with β, γ, δ, ζ, (λ), μ, ν, ϱ, e.g. *τῆς Μαϱίας* [tizmarias] *Mary's.*

When final ν is in contact with an initial stop consonant, the following changes result:

ν–κ [ng] *στόν κήπο* [stongipo] *in the garden.*
ν–μπ [mb] *ἄν μποϱῶ* [amboro] *if I can.*
ν–ξ [ngz] *σάν ξύλο* [sangzilo] *like wood.*
ν–π [mb] *δέν πειϱάζει* [dhembirazi] *it doesn't matter.*
ν–τ [nd] *ἐν τάξει* [endaksi] *all right.*
ν–τσ [ndz] *στήν τσάντα της* [stindzandatis] *in her bag.*
ν–ψ [mbz] *τῶν ψυχῶν* [tombzikhon] (*All*) *souls'* (*day*).

PRONUNCIATION EXERCISES

From page 30.

Ἡ μητέϱα εἶναι καλή.
[imitera ine kali.]

Τό ἁμάξι εἶναι πολύ μεγάλο.
[toamaksi ine poli meghalo.]

Ἡ νύχτα εἶναι θαυμάσια.
[inikta ine thavmasia.]

Τό μεγάλο μπάϱ εἶναι γεμᾶτο.
[tomeghalo bar ine yemato.]

Ὁ πατέϱας εἶναι πολύ καλός.
[opateras ine poli kalos.]

Εἶναι ἕνα ὡϱαῖο κοϱίτσι.
[ine enaoreo koritsi.]

Εἶναι μιά πολύ καλή μητέϱα.
[ine myapoli kali mitera.]

Εἶναι ἕνας πολύ καλός ἄνθϱωπος.
[ine enaspoli kalos anthropos.]

'Η ζωή εἶναι δύσκολη.
[izo*i* *i*ne dh*i*skoli.]

Τό πρωινό εἶναι ἕτοιμο.
[toproin*o* *i*ne *e*timo.]

From page 43.

Αὐτό τό δωμάτιο εἶναι δικό του.
[aft*o* todhom*a*tio *i*ne dhik*o*tu.]

Αὐτά εἶναι δικά μας παιδιά.
[aft*a* *i*ne dhik*a*mas pedhy*a*.]

Εἶναι δικό σας αὐτό τό καπέλλο;
[*i*ne dhik*o*sas aft*o* tokap*e*lo?]

Τό μεσημέρι ἦταν πολύ ζεστό.
[tomesim*e*ri *i*tan pol*i* zest*o*.]

Αὐτά τά τσιγάρα εἶναι δικά της.
[aft*a* tatsigh*a*ra *i*ne dhik*a*tis.]

'Η φωνή του εἶναι πολύ δυνατή.
[ifon*i*tu *i*ne pol*i* dhinat*i*.]

'Ο Γιῶργος εἶναι ἄνθρωπος δικός μας.
[oy*o*rghos *i*ne *a*nthropos dhik*o*zmas.]

Τά πόδια του εἶναι μεγάλα.
[tap*o*dhyatu *i*ne megh*a*la.]

Αὐτή εἶναι δική μου ὑπόθεσις.
[aft*i* *i*ne dhik*i*mu ip*o*thesis.]

Δέν εἶναι δουλειά δική σου.
[dh*e*n*i*ne dhuly*a* dhik*i*su.]

"Ολα αὐτά τά τσιγάρα εἶναι δικά σου;
[*o*la aft*a* tatsigh*a*ra *i*ne dhik*a*su?]

Ἡ καρδιά του εἶναι πολύ ζεστή.
[ikardhyatu ine poli zesti.]

From page 162.

Καλημέρα σας. Τί γίνεστε;
[Kalimerasas. ti yineste?

Πολύ καλά, εὐχαριστῶ, ἐσεῖς;
polikala efkharisto, esis?

Τά ἴδια. Πῶς πάει ἡ δουλειά; Ἡσυχία.
taidhia. pos pai idhulya? isikhia.

Εἶναι κρῖμα νά δουλεύει κανείς
ine krima nadhulevikanis

μ' ἕνα τόσο θαυμάσιο καιρό.
menatoso thavmasio kero.

Συμφωνῶ πληρέστατα. Τήν ἐρχόμενη
simfono plirestata. tinerkhomeni

ἑβδομάδα ὅμως ἔχουμε δυό μέρες ἄδεια.
evdhomadhaomos, ekhume dhyo meres adhia.

Τί γίνεται ὁ ἀδελφός σας; Καλά εἶναι.
ti yinete oadhelfossas? kalaine.

Τίς προάλλες μέ ρωτοῦσε γιά σένα.
tisproales merotuse yasena.

Νά τοῦ δόσεις πολλούς χαιρετισμούς. Ἀντίο.
natudhosis polus kheretizmus. adio.]

From page 166.

Μπορῶ νά μιλήσω στόν κύριον Ἀλέκο, παρακαλῶ;
[boro namiliso stongirion aleko, parakalo?

Ἕνα λεπτό παρακαλῶ. Ἐμπρός.
enalepto parakalo. embros.

'Ο κύριος 'Αλέκος; 'Ο ἴδιος.
ok*i*rios al*e*kos? o*i*dhios.

'Ο κύριος Πάνος ἐδῶ. Εἶναι γιά τήν ὑπόθεση
ok*i*rios p*a*nos edh*o*. *i*ne yatinip*o*thesi

τοῦ διαμερίσματος πού σᾶς ἀνάφερα
tudhiamer*i*zmatos pusasan*a*fera

τίς προάλλες. Μήπως ἔχετε κανένα
tispro*a*les. m*i*pos *e*khete kan*e*na

διαθέσιμο τώρα; Μιά στιγμή νά κοιτάξω,
dhiath*e*simo t*o*ra? my*a*stighm*i* nakit*a*kso,

κύριε Πάνο. 'Αλό. Εἶστε πολύ τυχερός,
k*i*rie p*a*no. al*o*. *i*ste pol*i* tikher*o*s,

κύριε Πάνο. Ἔχω ἀκριβῶς ἕνα
k*i*rie p*a*no. *e*kho akriv*o*s *e*na

πού σᾶς κάνει περίφημα. Πότε μπορεῖτε
pusask*a*ni per*i*fima. p*o*te bor*i*te

νά τό δεῖτε; Μπορῶ σήμερα ἤ αὔριο,
natodh*i*te? bor*o* s*i*mera i*a*vrio,

ἀλλά μετά τίς ἕξι. 'Εν τάξει. Θά σᾶς δόσω
al*a* met*a*tis*e*ksi. end*a*ksi. thasazdh*o*so

τή διεύθυνση, καί μπορεῖτε νά πᾶτε
tidhi*e*fthinsi, kebor*i*te nap*a*te

καί μόνος σας. Εὐχαριστῶ πολύ.
kem*o*nossas. efkharist*o* pol*i*.

Σᾶς εἶμαι πολύ ὑπόχρεος. 'Εγώ, εὐχαριστῶ.
sas*i*me pol*i* ip*o*khreos. egh*o*, efkharist*o*.]

PARTS OF SPEECH

Every language has its characteristic ways of adapting words to perform their appropriate task in the stream of speech. Grammar studies and describes these ways; and when we learn the grammar of a foreign language, we shall inevitably find a contrast between its ways of using words and the ways of English.

The first thing to notice about Greek is that it possesses more *variable* words than English. Variable words are those whose form is changed according to their function in a sentence. This change is usually called *inflexion*, and most often involves the use of different endings. English uses fewer inflexions, and relies more on other means of discrimination, such as word-order and the use of structural features like *to* and *of*. For example, in the sentences *the doctor came* and *he saw the doctor*, the Greek word for *doctor* (*γιατρός*) has a different ending in each phrase. *The doctor came* is *ὁ γιατρός ἦρθε*, while *he saw the doctor* is *εἶδε τό γιατρό*. This significant variation of the endings allows more freedom of word-order in Greek. Thus, *the doctor came* might also be *ἦρθε ὁ γιατρός*.

In Greek, variable words include nouns, pronouns, adjectives and verbs. *Invariable* words include prepositions, conjunctions, particles, etc.

Changes in the form of nouns are used to denote gender, number (singular or plural) and case (as in English *I* or *me*, *who* or *whose*). In pronouns they denote gender, number, case and person (*I*, *you* or *he*). In adjectives they denote gender, number, case and degree (big, bigg*er*, bigg*est*). In verbs they denote number, person and time.

PART ONE

VARIABLE WORDS

NOUNS

Greek nouns are divided into three classes or genders, which may be termed M, F and N, as these classes are also called masculine, feminine and neuter.*

M nouns are those which can be preceded by the article *ὁ*, e.g. *ὁ ἄνθρωπος*, the man; *ὁ πατέρας*, the father; *ὁ Γιάννης*, John.
Their indefinite article is *ἕνας*, e.g. *ἕνας ἄνθρωπος*, a man; *ἕνας κῆπος*, a garden.

F nouns are those which can be preceded by the article *ἡ*, e.g. *ἡ πόρτα*, the door; *ἡ ζωή*, life; *ἡ γυναίκα*, the woman.
Their indefinite article is *μιά*, e.g. *μιά γυναίκα*, a woman; *μιά ἱστορία*, a story.

N nouns are those which can be preceded by the article *τό*, e.g. *τό γραφεῖο*, the office; *τό παιδί*, the child; *τό μπάρ*, the bar.
Their indefinite article is *ἕνα*, e.g. *ἕνα παιδί*, a child; *ἕνα δωμάτιο*, a room.

Nouns are divided into the following main sub-classes according to their endings:

The nouns of class M end mostly in:

M_1 *-ος*, e.g. *ὁ ἄνθρωπος*, the man

Some end in:

M_2 *-ας*, e.g. *ὁ πατέρας*, the father
M_3 *-ης*, e.g. *ὁ ἐργάτης*, the workman

* There is some correlation of gender with sex.

The nouns of class F end in:

F_1 -η, e.g. *ἡ ἀδελφή*, the sister
F_2 -α, e.g. *ἡ γυναίκα*, the woman

The nouns of class N end mostly in:

N_1 -ο, e.g. *τό γραφεῖο*, the office
N_2 -ι, e.g. *τό παιδί*, the child

Some end in:

N_3 -α, e.g. *τό ὄνομα*, the name
N_4 in different other sounds, e.g. *τό μπάρ*, the bar; *τό γκαράζ*, the garage; *τό φῶς*, the light; *τό τέλος*, the end.

Note that the article *ὁ*, *ἡ*, *τό* may be used even in front of proper names and abstract nouns, e.g. *ὁ Γιάννης*, John; *ἡ Ἀγγλία*, England; *ὁ Αὔγουστος*, August; *ἡ ζωή*, life; *ἡ χαρά*, joy.

ADJECTIVES

Adjectives can take three endings corresponding to the three classes of nouns. Thus " good " can be (M) *καλός*, (F) *καλή*, (N) *καλό* according to the noun with which it is used, e.g.

M. *ὁ καλός ἄνθρωπος*, the good man
F. *ἡ καλή γυναίκα*, the good woman
N. *τό καλό παιδί*, the good child

M. *ὁ μεγάλος κῆπος*, the big garden
F. *ἡ μεγάλη πόρτα*, the big door
N. *τό μεγάλο δωμάτιο*, the big room

The three forms of the adjectives end mostly in

M -ος, e.g. *καλός*
F -η, e.g. *καλή*
N -ο, e.g. *καλό*

Some have their F form ending in *-α*, e.g.

ἡ θαυμάσια μητέρα, the wonderful mother
ἡ καινούρια ζωή, the new life
ἡ ὡραία ἱστορία, the nice story
ἡ πλούσια γυναίκα, the rich woman

These are the adjectives which have a vowel (mainly *ι*) before the last vowel.

VOCABULARY

ἡ γυναίκα, woman
ὁ ἄνθρωπος, man
ἡ νύχτα, night
ἡ ζωή, life
τό πρωϊνό, breakfast
ὁ κῆπος, garden
ἡ μητέρα, mother
τό ἁμάξι, car
τό μπάρ, bar
πολύ, very
ἡ Μαρία, Mary
τό κορίτσι, girl
ὡραῖος, beautiful
δροσερός, cool
δύσκολος, difficult
ἕτοιμος, ready
θαυμάσιος, wonderful
καλός, good
καινούριος, new
γεμᾶτος, full
εἶναι, is, are (he, she, it) is, they are

EXAMPLES

Ὁ κῆπος εἶναι μεγάλος, The garden is big.
Ἡ ζωή εἶναι δύσκολη,* Life is difficult.
Τό πρωϊνό εἶναι ἕτοιμο, Breakfast is ready.
Τό μπάρ εἶναι γεμᾶτο, The bar is full.
Τό ἁμάξι εἶναι καινούριο, The car is new.
Ἡ νύχτα εἶναι δροσερή, The night is cool.
Ἡ μητέρα εἶναι πολύ καλή, Mother is very good.

* This, and many similar sentences, could also be expressed in a different word-order, e.g. *Δύσκολη εἶναι ἡ ζωή*. In general, there is more flexibility in word-order in Greek than there is in English.

Ὁ ἄνθρωπος εἶναι καλός, The man is good.
Ἡ Μαρία εἶναι ἕνα θαυμάσιο κορίτσι, Mary is a wonderful girl.
Εἶναι μιά ὡραία γυναίκα, She is a beautiful woman.
Εἶναι μιά πολύ καλή μητέρα, She is a very good mother.
Ὁ κῆπος εἶναι πολύ μεγάλος, The garden is very big.
Τό καινούριο ἁμάξι εἶναι μεγάλο, The new car is big.
Ἡ ζωή εἶναι ὡραία, Life is beautiful.
Ἡ δροσερή νύχτα εἶναι θαυμάσια, The cool night is wonderful.

EXERCISE 1

Translate:

1. *Ἡ μητέρα εἶναι καλή.*
2. *Τό ἁμάξι εἶναι πολύ μεγάλο.*
3. *Ἡ νύχτα εἶναι θαυμάσια.*
4. *Τό μεγάλο μπάρ εἶναι γεμᾶτο.*
5. *Ὁ πατέρας εἶναι πολύ καλός.*
6. *Εἶναι ἕνα ὡραῖο κορίτσι.*
7. *Εἶναι μιά πολύ καλή μητέρα.*
8. *Εἶναι ἕνας πολύ καλός ἄνθρωπος.*
9. *Ἡ ζωή εἶναι δύσκολη.*
10. *Τό πρωϊνό εἶναι ἕτοιμο.*

'THIS' AND 'THAT'

The adjectivals* *αὐτός*, this, and *ἐκεῖνος*, that, change their endings according to the class of the nouns with which they are used.

When they are followed by a noun the definite article is always inserted between them. Thus:

M *Αὐτός ὁ ἄνθρωπος*, This man
Αὐτός ὁ κῆπος, This garden
F *Αὐτή ἡ γυναίκα*, This woman
Αὐτή ἡ ζωή, This life
N *Αὐτό τό παιδί*, This child
Αὐτό τό ἁμάξι, This car

M *'Εκεῖνος ὁ ἐργάτης*, That worker
F *'Εκείνη ἡ νύχτα*, That night
N *'Εκεῖνο τό δωμάτιο*, That room

Αὐτός ὁ ἄνθρωπος εἶναι πολύ καλός, This man is very good
'Εκείνη ἡ γυναίκα εἶναι ὡραία, That woman is beautiful
Αὐτό τό μπάρ εἶναι γεμᾶτο, This bar is full

EXERCISE 2

Fill in the blanks:

1. *Αὐτό τό παιδί εἶναι καλ–*
2. *'Η νύχτα εἶναι δροσερ–*
3. *'Εκεῖν– τό ἁμάξι εἶναι μεγάλο.*
4. *Εἶναι ἕνας πολύ καλ– πατέρας.*
5. *Αὐτ– ἡ γυναίκα εἶναι ὡραία.*

* The term adjectival is used for adjectives which are use in special ways.

6. *Τό πρωϊνό – ἕτοιμο.*
7. *'Εκεῖν– ὁ κῆπος εἶναι μεγάλ–*
8. *'Η ζωή εἶναι δύσκολ–*
9. *Τό μπάρ εἶναι γεμᾶτ–*
10. *Αὐτή ἡ ἱστορία εἶναι θαυμάσι–*
11. *Εἶναι ἕνα θαυμάσι– κορίτσι.*
12. *Αὐτός ὁ —*
13. *Αὐτή ἡ —*
14. *Αὐτό τό —*

Negation is expressed by putting the negative particle *δέν* in front of the verb, e.g. *Τό πρωϊνό εἶναι ἕτοιμο,* Breakfast is ready. *Τό πρωϊνό δέν εἶναι ἕτοιμο,* Breakfast is not ready. *Τό μπάρ δέν εἶναι γεμᾶτο,* The bar is not full. *Αὐτή ἡ πόρτα δέν εἶναι μεγάλη,* This door is not big.

VOCABULARY

ἦταν, was, were (he, she, it) was, they were
νέος, new, young
ἡ κοπέλλα, girl
τό πάρτυ, party
εὐτυχισμένος, happy
ὑπέροχος, wonderful
σωστός, correct
πλούσιος, rich
ὁ φιλόσοφος, philosopher
λίγο, a little
σοβαρός, serious
λυπημένος, sad
δέν, not
ἀνόητος, silly
τό καμπαρέ, night-club

EXAMPLES

Εἶναι ἕνα θαυμάσιο παιδί, He is a wonderful boy.
'Η γυναίκα ἦταν λυπημένη, The woman was sad.
Αὐτός ὁ ἄνθρωπος εἶναι πολύ σοβαρός, This man is very serious.
Τό πάρτυ ἦταν ὑπέροχο, The party was wonderful.

'Η νέα κοπέλλα δέν εἶναι εὐτυχισμένη, The young girl is not happy.
Αὐτό δέν εἶναι σωστό, This is not right.
Εἶναι πολύ ἀνόητο, It is very silly.
Αὐτό τό παιδί εἶναι εὐτυχισμένο, This boy is happy.
'Ο Γιῶργος εἶναι πολύ πλούσιος, George is very rich.
'Ο Γιάννης εἶναι λίγο λυπημένος, John is a little sad.

EXERCISE 3

Translate:

1. *'Εκείνη ἡ γυναίκα ἦταν πολύ ὡραία.*
2. *Αὐτό τό παιδί εἶναι πολύ εὐτυχισμένο.*
3. *Τό καμπαρέ δέν ἦταν γεμᾶτο.*
4. *'Ο Γιῶργος εἶναι πολύ ἀνόητος.*
5. *'Η ζωή εἶναι ὡραία.*
6. *'Η μητέρα εἶναι μιά πολύ καλή γυναίκα.*
7. *'Ο πατέρας εἶναι ἕνας θαυμάσιος ἄνθρωπος.*
8. *'Η Μαρία ἦταν πολύ σοβαρή.*
9. *Αὐτός ὁ κῆπος δέν εἶναι μεγάλος.*
10. *Αὐτό δέν εἶναι σωστό.*
11. *'Ο Ράσσελ εἶναι ἕνας μεγάλος φιλόσοφος.*
12. *'Ο Πλάτων ἦταν ἕνας μεγάλος φιλόσοφος.*

THE PLURAL OF NOUNS

Nouns form their plural in these ways:

1. Nouns of the first class (M) by changing
   (i) The article *ὁ* into *οἱ*
   (ii) M_1. The ending *-ος* into *-οι*, e.g. *ὁ ἄνθρωπος*, the man; *οἱ ἄνθρωποι*, the men.
   $M_{2, 3}$. The ending *-ας* or *-ης* into *-ες*, e.g. *ὁ ἄντρας*, the man; *οἱ ἄντρες*, the men; *ὁ ἐργάτης*, the worker; *οἱ ἐργάτες*,* the workers.

2. Nouns of the second class (F) by changing
   (i) The article *ἡ* into *οἱ*
   (ii) F_1 and F_2. The ending *-η* or *-α* into *-ες*, e.g. *ἡ ἀδελφή*, the sister; *οἱ ἀδελφές*, the sisters; *ἡ μέρα*, the day; *οἱ μέρες*, the days.

Some nouns of sub-class F_1 change the final *-η* into *-εις*, e.g. *ἡ λέξη*, the word; *οἱ λέξεις*, the words; *ἡ σκέψη*, the thought; *οἱ σκέψεις*, the thoughts. Such words may also be written with a final *-ις* in the singular, e.g. *ἡ λέξις*, *ἡ σκέψις*.

3. Nouns of the third class (N) by changing
   (i) The article *τό* into *τά*
   (ii) N_1. The ending *-ο* into *-α*, e.g. *τό τσιγάρο*, the cigarette; *τά τσιγάρα*, the cigarettes.
   N_2. The ending *-ι* into *-ια*, e.g. *τό ἁμάξι*, the car; *τά ἁμάξια*, the cars.

* Most nouns ending in *-άς* or *-ής* (accented) form the plural by changing the final *ς* into *-δες*, e.g. *ὁ παπάς*, priest; *οἱ παπάδες*, priests.

N_3. The ending -*α* into -*ατα*, e.g. *τό χρῶμα*, the colour; *τά χρώματα*, the colours.

Note that *τό μπάρ*, plural = *τά μπάρ*, *τό καμπαρέ*, pl. = *τά καμπαρέ*, *τό φῶς*, light, pl. = *τά φῶτα*.

THE PLURAL OF ADJECTIVES

Adjectives associated with nouns in the plural also change their endings. In general, there is complete concord between the forms of nouns and adjectives. That is, every change in the endings of nouns is accompanied by a corresponding change in the endings of adjectives. Adjectives form their plural by undergoing the same final changes as the main noun forms. Thus, they change the ending:

(M) *-ος* into *-οι*
(F) *-η* or *-α* into *-ες*
(N) *-ο* into *-α*

E.g. (M) *Ὁ καλός ἄνθρωπος*, The good man.
Οἱ καλοί ἄνθρωποι, The good men.
Ὁ ἄνθρωπος εἶναι καλός, The man is good.
Οἱ ἄνθρωποι εἶναι καλοί, The men are good.
(F) *Ἡ καλή γυναίκα*, The good woman.
Οἱ καλές γυναῖκες, The good women.
Ἡ γυναίκα εἶναι καλή, The woman is good.
Οἱ γυναῖκες εἶναι καλές, The women are good.
(N) *Τό καλό παιδί*, The good child.
Τά καλά παιδιά, The good children.
Τό παιδί εἶναι καλό, The child is good.
Τά παιδιά εἶναι καλά, The children are good.

Note that some nouns are more common in the plural than in the singular form, e.g. *τά μαλλιά*, the hair; *τά χείλη*, the lips; *τά λεφτά*, the money; *τά λόγια*, words, talk; *τά δάκρυα*, tears.

VOCABULARY

καί, and
δύο or *δυό*, two
ἄλλος, other
ἀπαραίτητος, necessary, indispensable
νεαρός, young man
τό ψέμα, the lie
ἡ Ἀθήνα, Athens
πράσινος, green
μαῦρος, black
ἡ συνέπεια, consequence
ἡ μέρα, day
τό δωμάτιο, room
κακός, bad
ξανθός, blond, fair
τό χρῶμα, colour
ἐδῶ, here
μακρυά, far
τό νερό water
κρύος, cold

EXERCISE 4

Translate:

1. *Οἱ νύχτες εἶναι δροσερές.*
2. *Οἱ μέρες δέν εἶναι πολύ δροσερές.*
3. *Οἱ συνέπειες ἦταν σοβαρές.*
4. *Τά λεφτά εἶναι ἀπαραίτητα.*
5. *Αὐτοί οἱ νεαροί εἶναι εὐτυχισμένοι.*
6. *Δυό πράσινα μάτια.*
7. *Κακά εἶναι τά ψέματα.*
8. *Τά μαῦρα μάτια εἶναι ὡραῖα.*
9. *Ἡ Ἀθήνα εἶναι μαγευτική.*
10. *Ἕνα παιδί ἦταν ἐδῶ. Τά ἄλλα παιδιά ἦταν πολύ μακρυά.*
11. *Αὐτά τά δυό δωμάτια εἶναι μεγάλα καί δροσερά.*
12. *Οἱ ἄνθρωποι, οἱ γυναῖκες καί τά παιδιά εἶναι εὐτυχισμένοι.*
13. *Τά πολλά λεφτά δέν εἶναι ἀπαραίτητα.*
14. *Τά ξανθά μαλλιά εἶναι ὡραῖα.*
15. *Ἡ ἄλλη γυναῖκα δέν ἦταν πολύ καλή.*
16. *Αὐτό τό χρῶμα εἶναι πράσινο.*
17. *Αὐτό τό νερό εἶναι κρύο.*

EXERCISE 5

Fill in the blanks:

1. *Τά μεγάλ– δωμάτια.*
2. *οἱ ἄλλ– ἄντρες.*
3. *ὁ σοβαρ– ἄνθρωπος.*
4. *ἕνα πράσιν– ἁμάξι.*
5. *μιά θαυμάσι– ἱστορία.*
6. *οἱ ὡραῖ– γυναῖκες.*
7. *τά μαῦρ– μαλλιά.*
8. *ἡ μαγευτικ– Ἀθήνα.*
9. *μιά δύσκολ– ζωή.*
10. *τά ὡραῖ– χείλη.*

THE PRONOUNS 'MY', 'YOUR', ETC.

The personal pronouns expressing possession are changed for person and number as follows:

	Singular	*Plural*
1.	*μου*, my	*μας*, our
2.	*σου*, your	*σας*, your
3.	*του*, his	*τους*, their
	της, her	
	του, its	

These pronouns are put after the nouns with which they are associated. The nouns are preceded by the article, e.g.

τό σπίτι, the house
τό σπίτι μου, my house
τό ὄνομα, the name
τό ὄνομά μου, my name
ὁ φίλος, the friend
ὁ φίλος μας, our friend
ἡ οἰκογένεια, the family
ἡ οἰκογένειά τους, their family

τό χέρι μου, my hand; *ὁ πατέρας σου*, your father; *ἡ μητέρα της*, her mother; *ὁ κῆπος μας*, our garden; *οἱ κῆποι μας*, our gardens; *τά λεφτά σας*, your money.

When the nouns are preceded by an adjective the possessive pronoun is usually put between the adjective and the noun, e.g.

τό ἁμάξι, the car
τό καινούριο ἁμάξι, the new car

τό καινούριο μου ἁμάξι, my new car
τά μαῦρα μαλλιά, the black hair
τά μαῦρα της μαλλιά, her black hair

Ἡ καλή μου μητέρα, my good mother; *τό μεγάλο της παιδί*, her big child; *ὁ καλός μας φίλος*, our good friend; *ὁ καλός σας φίλος*, your good friend; *οἱ καλοί σας φίλοι*, your good friends; *τά μεγάλα τους σπίτια*, their big houses.

Sometimes the pronoun is put after the noun, e.g. *οἱ καλοί φίλοι μας*, our good friends; *τά μαῦρα μαλλιά σου*, your black hair; *τά ὡραῖα μάτια της*, her beautiful eyes.

VOCABULARY

ἡ ἀδελφή, sister
τό πρόσωπο, face
ἡ θεία, aunt
τό ποτήρι, glass
φτωχός, poor
ἀλλά, but
ἡ οἰκογένεια, family

ὁ ἀδελφός, brother
ὁ θεῖος, uncle
τό κεφάλι, head
μικρός, small
λεπτός, thin
μπλέ, blue
δυνατός, strong

EXAMPLES

Τό ὄνομά μου εἶναι Ἀντρέας, My name is Andrew.
Ὁ ἀδελφός μου καί ὁ πατέρας σου εἶναι φίλοι, My brother and your father are friends.
Τό πρόσωπό του ἦταν πολύ σοβαρό, His face was very serious.
Τά μάτια της εἶναι μαῦρα, Her eyes are black.
Ἡ οἰκογένειά του εἶναι πλούσια, His family is rich.
Ὁ πατέρας σου εἶναι καλός ἄνθρωπος, Your (sing.) father is a good man.
Τό ποτήρι του ἦταν γεμᾶτο, His glass was full.

EXERCISE 6

Translate:

1. *Ἡ ἀδελφή σου εἶναι λυπημένη.*
2. *Ὁ θεῖος μας εἶναι πολύ καλός ἀλλά εἶναι φτωχός.*
3. *Τά χέρια τους εἶναι μαῦρα.*
4. *Ἡ θεία μου ἦταν πολύ εὐτυχισμένη.*
5. *Τό κεφάλι του εἶναι λίγο μικρό.*
6. *Τά μαλλιά της εἶναι ξανθά καί τά μάτια της μπλέ.*
7. *Τό καινούριο του ἁμάξι εἶναι μαῦρο.*
8. *Τό σπίτι μου εἶναι μικρό ἀλλά δροσερό.*
9. *Ὁ ἀδελφός μου εἶναι λεπτός ἀλλά πολύ δυνατός.*
10. *Ὁ Γιῶργος εἶναι φίλος μου ἀλλά ὁ Γιάννης δέν εἶναι.*
11. *Ἡ οἰκογένεια του εἶναι φτωχή.*
12. *Τά χέρια της εἶναι λεπτά.*

THE PRONOUNS 'MINE', 'YOURS', ETC.

The personal pronouns corresponding to the English mine, yours, *or* my own, your own, etc. are formed by the adjective *δικός*, *δική*, *δικό*, followed by the pronoun *μου*, *σου*, etc.

The adjective changes according to the form of its noun. The adjective for nouns of class M is *δικός*, for class F *δική* and for class N *δικό*.

In the following paradigm *δικός* is used as the basic form.

Singular	*Plural*
δικός μου, mine	*δικός μας*, ours
δικός σου, yours	*δικός σας*, yours
δικός του, his	*δικός τους*, theirs
δικός της, hers	

EXAMPLES

Αὐτό τό σπίτι εἶναι δικό του, This house is his.
Αὐτό τό ὄνομα δέν εἶναι δικό σου, This name is not yours.
Εἶναι δικά μου τά λεφτά, The money is mine.
Τό δικό μας ἀμάξι εἶναι μικρό, Our own car is small.
Ὁ Ἀντρέας εἶναι δικός μου φίλος, Andrew is my own friend.
Αὐτά τά τσιγάρα εἶναι δικά της, These cigarettes are hers.

Note the implications of the above pronouns by themselves: *δικός μου* implies " mine, one object of class M "; *δικοί μου*, " mine, several objects of class M; *δικά του*, " his, several objects of class N ", etc.

Questions are denoted simply by intonation without any change in word-order, e.g.

'Η Μαρία εἶναι ἀδελφή σας; Is Mary your sister?
Αὐτό τό ποτήρι εἶναι δικό σας; Is this glass yours?
Ναί, Yes.
"Οχι, No.

VOCABULARY

ἡ δουλειά, work
τό πόδι, foot, leg
ὅλος, all
ζεστός, warm, hot
τό καπέλλο, hat
τό μεσημέρι, noon, mid-day
ἡ φωνή, voice
ἡ ὑπόθεσις, the matter
ἡ καρδιά, heart

EXERCISE 7

Translate:

1. *Αὐτό τό δωμάτιο εἶναι δικό του.*
2. *Αὐτά εἶναι δικά μας παιδιά.*
3. *Εἶναι δικό σας αὐτό τό καπέλλο;*
4. *Τό μεσημέρι ἦταν πολύ ζεστό.*
5. *Αὐτά τά τσιγάρα εἶναι δικά της.*
6. *'Η φωνή του εἶναι πολύ δυνατή.*
7. *'Ο Γιῶργος εἶναι ἄνθρωπος δικός μας.*
8. *Τά πόδια του εἶναι μεγάλα.*
9. *Αὐτή εἶναι δική μου ὑπόθεσις.*
10. *Δέν εἶναι δουλειά δική σου.*
11. *"Ολα αὐτά τά τσιγάρα εἶναι δικά σου;*
12. *'Η καρδιά του εἶναι πολύ ζεστή.*

GENITIVE OF NOUNS AND ADJECTIVES

Both nouns and adjectives change their form to denote singular or plural number and also to denote case according to their place and function in the sentence. Besides the nominative case that we have been considering as basic, they have two other forms in each number; the genitive and the accusative.

The genitive singular of nouns is formed by changing:

1. (M) The article *ὁ* into *τοῦ* (the indefinite article *ἕνας* into *ἑνός*).
   (F) The article *ἡ* into *τῆς* (the indefinite *μιά* into *μιᾶς*).
   (N) The article *τό* into *τοῦ* (the indefinite *ἕνα* into *ἑνός*).
2. M_1. The ending *-ος* into *-ου*, e.g. *ὁ θεῖος*, gen. *τοῦ θείου*; *ὁ κῆπος*, gen. *τοῦ κήπου.*
   M_2. The ending *-ας* into *-α*, e.g. *ὁ ἄντρας*, gen. *τοῦ ἄντρα.*
   M_3. The ending *-ης* into *-η*, e.g. *ὁ Γιάννης*, gen. *τοῦ Γιάννη.*
   F_1. The ending *-η* into *-ης*, e.g. *ἡ ἀδελφή*, gen. *τῆς ἀδελφῆς.*
   F_2. The ending *-α* into *-ας*, e.g. *ἡ μητέρα*, gen. *τῆς μητέρας.*
   N_1. The ending *-ο* into *-ου*, e.g. *τό τσιγάρο*, gen. *τοῦ τσιγάρου.*
   N_2. The ending *-ι* into *-ιοῦ*, e.g. *τό παιδί*, gen. *τοῦ παιδιοῦ.*
   N_3. The ending *-α* into *-ατος*, e.g. *τό ὄνομα*, gen. *τοῦ ὀνόματος.*

The genitive singular of adjectives is formed by changing the endings in the same way.

Thus:

M. *ὁ μεγάλος*, gen. *τοῦ μεγάλου*
F. *ἡ μεγάλη*, gen. *τῆς μεγάλης*
N. *τό μεγάλο*, gen. *τοῦ μεγάλου*

The accent may be removed to the following syllable in some nouns of sub-class M_1 and N_1, e.g. *ὁ ἄνθρωπος*, gen. *τοῦ ἀνθρώπου*; *τό δωμάτιο*, gen. *τοῦ δωματίου*; and in all nouns of sub-class N_2, e.g. *τό πόδι*, gen. *τοῦ ποδιοῦ*.

Adjectives have always the case of the nouns they qualify.

EXAMPLES

M.	*ὁ πλούσιος θεῖος*	gen.	*τοῦ πλούσιου θείου*
	ὁ νεαρός φίλος	„	*τοῦ νεαροῦ φίλου*
	ὁ ἄλλος ἄντρας	„	*τοῦ ἄλλου ἄντρα*
F.	*ἡ μικρή ἀδελφή*	„	*τῆς μικρῆς ἀδελφῆς*
	ἡ καλή μητέρα	„	*τῆς καλῆς μητέρας*
N.	*τό μεγάλο δωμάτιο*	„	*τοῦ μεγάλου δωματίου*
	τό μαῦρο ἁμάξι	„	*τοῦ μαύρου ἁμαξιοῦ*
	τό ξανθό χρῶμα	„	*τοῦ ξανθοῦ χρώματος*

The use of the genitive

The genitive is generally used to express possession or appurtenance, e.g.

Τό ὄνομα τοῦ πατέρα μου εἶναι Βασίλης, The name of my father is Basil.

'Ο ἀδελφός μου εἶναι φίλος τοῦ Γιώργου, My brother is a friend of George's.

'Η πόρτα τοῦ σπιτιοῦ μου εἶναι μαύρη, The door of my house is black.

Τό πάρτυ τοῦ Κώστα ἦταν ὑπέροχο, Costas' party was wonderful.

Τό χρῶμα τοῦ ἁμαξιοῦ του εἶναι μπλέ, The colour of his car is blue.

Τό ὄνομα τῆς μητέρας τοῦ φίλου μου εἶναι Μαρία, The name of my friend's mother is Mary.

Ἡ ζωή τῆς Ἀθήνας εἶναι δύσκολη, Life in Athens is difficult.

Ἡ ἀγάπη μιᾶς μητέρας εἶναι πολύ μεγάλη, A mother's love is very great.

Τό σπίτι ἑνός φτωχοῦ ἀνθρώπου εἶναι μικρό, The house of a poor man is small.

Τά μάτια μιᾶς ξανθῆς γυναίκας εἶναι μπλέ, A blond woman's eyes are blue.

VOCABULARY

ἡ μηχανή, engine	*εὐχάριστος,* pleasant
ὁ ἥλιος, sun	*κατάμαυρος,* very black
ὁ κύριος, Mr., gentleman	*ἡ μάνα,* mother
ἡ κυρία, Mrs., lady	*ἡ ἄνοιξη,* spring
ὁ Ἄγγλος, Englishman	*τό Αἰγαῖο,* Aegean
ἡ Ἀγγλίδα, Englishwoman	*τό αὐτοκίνητο,* car

EXERCISE 8

Translate:

1. *Τό σπίτι τῆς ἀδελφῆς μου εἶναι πολύ μεγάλο.*
2. *Ὁ κῆπος τοῦ σπιτιοῦ μας εἶναι μικρός ἀλλά ὡραῖος.*
3. *Τό ὄνομα αὐτοῦ τοῦ Ἄγγλου εἶναι Τζών.*
4. *Τό ὄνομα αὐτῆς τῆς Ἀγγλίδας εἶναι Μάρκρετ.*
5. *Τό πάρτυ τῆς κυρίας Μπενάκη ἦταν θαυμάσιο.*
6. *Ὁ ἥλιος τοῦ μεσημεριοῦ εἶναι πολύ ζεστός.*
7. *Τά μαλλιά τοῦ Ἀντρέα εἶναι μαῦρα.*

8. *Ἡ οἰκογένεια τοῦ κυρίου Ἀντώνη εἰναι πολύ πλούσια.*
9. *Τό φῶς τοῦ μικροῦ σου δωματίου δέν εἶναι πολύ δυνατό.*
10. *Ἡ ἄνοιξη τῆς Ἀθήνας εἶναι μαγευτική.*
11. *Ὁ ἥλιος τοῦ Αἰγαίου εἶναι ζεστός καί εὐχάριστος.*
12. *Τά μάτια αὐτῆς τῆς γυναίκας εἶναι κατάμαυρα.*
13. *Τό γραφεῖο τοῦ φίλου μου εἶναι λίγο μικρό, ἀλλά δροσερό καί εὐχάριστο.*
14. *Ἡ μηχανή τοῦ αὐτοκινήτου σου εἶναι πολύ δυνατή.*
15. *Τά μαλλιά τῆς νέας ἐκείνης Ἀγγλίδας εἶναι ξανθά.*

GENITIVE PLURAL

The genitive plural is a rather rare case. It is formed by changing:

1. all articles into *τῶν*.
2. the final syllable of the nominative plural into *-ων*.

The accent may be removed to the following syllable in some nouns of sub-classes M_1, F_1 and N_1; in most M_3 and N_3; and in all M_2 and N_2 nouns, e.g.

	Nominative Plural	*Genitive Plural*
M_1.	*οἱ ἄνθρωποι*	*τῶν ἀνθρώπων*
M_3.	*οἱ ἐργάτες*	*τῶν ἐργατῶν*
F_2.	*οἱ γυναῖκες*	*τῶν γυναικῶν*
F_1.	*οἱ ἀδελφές*	*τῶν ἀδελφῶν*
N_1.	*τά γραφεῖα*	*τῶν γραφείων*
N_2.	*τά πόδια*	*τῶν ποδιῶν*
N_3.	*τά ὀνόματα*	*τῶν ὀνομάτων*

The nouns of sub-class F_1, whose nominative plural ends in *-εις*, change this ending into *-εων*, e.g. *οἱ λέξεις*, gen. *τῶν λέξεων*; *οἱ σκέψεις*, gen. *τῶν σκέψεων*. Such words may also form their genitive singular in *-εως*, e.g. nominative *ἡ σκέψη* or *ἡ σκέψις*, gen. *τῆς σκέψης* or *τῆς σκέψεως*.

Like the nouns, adjectives form their genitive plural by changing the endings of the nominative plural into *-ων*, e.g.

	Nominative Plural	*Genitive Plural*
M.	*καλοί*	*καλῶν*
F.	*καλές*	*καλῶν*
N.	*καλά*	*καλῶν*

VOCABULARY

ἕνας, one (used with nouns of class M), gen. *ἑνός*
μιά, one (used with nouns of class F), gen. *μιᾶς*
ἕνα,* one (used with nouns of class N), gen. *ἑνός*
δύο, two
τρεῖς, three (with nouns of class M and F), gen. *τριῶν*
τρία, three (with nouns of class N), gen. *τριῶν*
τέσσερεις, four (with nouns of class M and F), gen. *τεσσάρων*
τέσσερα, four (with nouns of class N), gen. *τεσσάρων*

πέντε, five
ἕξι, six
ἑφτά, seven
ὀκτώ, eight
ἐννιά, nine
δέκα, ten
ὁ χρόνος, year
συγκινητικός, moving
τό δέντρο, tree
σκληρός, hard
μόνο, only
πράσινος, green

EXAMPLES

'Ο μικρός Γιῶργος εἶναι πέντε χρονῶν, Little George is five years old.
'Η Μαρία εἶναι ἑφτά χρονῶν, Mary is seven.
Τό χρῶμα τῶν δέντρων εἶναι πράσινο, The colour of the trees is green.
Τό χρῶμα τῶν ματιῶν τοῦ Νίκου εἶναι μπλέ, The colour of Nikos' eyes is blue.
'Η ζωή τῶν πλούσιων ἀνθρώπων εἶναι εὐχάριστη, The life of rich men is pleasant.

* The numerals *ἕνας, τρεῖς, τέσσερεις* can be considered as adjectivals in that they vary to express gender, e.g. *ἕνας ἀδελφός*, a brother; *μιά ἀδελφή*, a sister; *ἕνα παιδί*, a boy, etc.

EXERCISE 9

Translate:

1. *Τά δωμάτια τῶν μεγάλων σπιτιῶν εἶναι δροσερά.*
2. *Ἡ ζωή τῶν ἐργατῶν εἶναι σκληρή.*
3. *Ὁ ἀδελφός μου εἶναι μόνο ὀκτώ χρονῶν.*
4. *Οἱ μηχανές τῶν καλῶν αὐτοκινήτων εἶναι δυνατές.*
5. *Ἡ μικρή μου ἀδελφή εἶναι τεσσάρων χρονῶν.*
6. *Τά χέρια τῶν ὡραίων γυναικῶν εἶναι λεπτά.*
7. *Ἡ ἱστορία τῶν τριῶν παιδιῶν καί τῆς φτωχῆς μάνας τους ἦταν πολύ συγκινητική.*

THE ACCUSATIVE

A very frequent case is the accusative singular which is formed by changing:

1. M. The article ὁ into τό (the indefinite article ἕνας into ἕνα).
   F. The article ἡ into τή.
   N. The article τό into τό.
2. M_1. The ending *-ος* into *-ο*.
   M_2. The ending *-ας* into *-α*.
   M_3. The ending *-ης* into *-η*.

All other endings remain unchanged except the class F ending *-ος* which changes into *-ο*. (See p. 55.)

A final *ν* is added to both articles of class M and F, as well as to most nouns and adjectives of class M and F, when the following word begins with a vowel or *κ, π, τ, ξ, ψ*.

EXAMPLES

	Nominative	*Accusative*
M_1.	ὁ ἄνθρωπος	τόν ἄνθρωπο
	ὁ καλός ἄνθρωπος	τόν καλόν ἄνθρωπο
M_2.	ὁ πατέρας	τόν πατέρα
M_3.	ὁ Γιάννης	τό Γιάννη
F_1.	ἡ ζωή	τή ζωή
	ἡ ὡραία ζωή	τήν ὡραία ζωή
F_2.	ἡ πόρτα	τήν πόρτα

The accusative is used:

1. After prepositions such as *σέ*, to, on to, into, at, etc.;

μέ, with; *πάνω σέ*, on; *κοντά σέ*, near; *μέσα σέ*, into, inside; *ἀπό*, from; *πάνω ἀπό*, over; *κάτω ἀπό*, under; *γιά*, for, etc. The preposition *σέ* becomes *σ* in front of the articles which begin with *τ* or a vowel. In the case of *τ* the *σ* is written jointly with the article, e.g. *στόν πατέρα, στή μητέρα, στό γραφεῖο, κοντά στόν κῆπο.* Otherwise it is written as *σ'*, e.g. *σ' ἕνα σινεμά.*

2. After verbs such as *βλέπω*, I see; *τρώγω*, I eat; *θέλω*, I want; *ἔχω*, I have, etc.; e.g. *Βλέπω ἕναν ἄνθρωπο*, I see a man; *Ἔχω τρεῖς ἀδελφούς*, I have three brothers; *Θέλω δέκα τσιγάρα*, I want ten cigarettes.
3. After some nouns when it expresses their content, e.g. *ἕνα ποτήρι νερό*, a glass of water.

VOCABULARY

ἡ Ἰταλία, Italy
ἡ Ἑλλάδα, Greece
κάμποσος (adj.), a lot
τά λεφτά, money
τό σαλόνι, living room
γκρίζος, grey
ἡ Κύπρος, Cyprus
τό μπουκάλι, bottle
τό ἀεροπλάνο, airplane
ἡ Ἀμερική, America
ἦρθε, he came
ἔχω, I have
πολλοί (adj. pl.), a lot
ἡ Ἀγγλία, England
ἡ ὥρα, hour, time
τό κρασί, wine
ἡ θάλασσα, sea
τό νερό, water
ἡ βεράντα, veranda
ὅλος, whole
ψηλός, high, tall
δόσε μου, give me
εἶδε, he saw
θέλω, I want
ὅλοι, all

EXAMPLES

Ὁ πατέρας του εἶναι στήν Ἰταλία, His father is in Italy.
Ἦρθε στήν Ἑλλάδα μέ κάμποσα λεφτά, He came to Greece with a lot of money.

Αὐτήν τήν ὥρα εἶναι στό ἀεροπλάνο, At this time he is in the airplane.
Ὁ θεῖος μου εἶναι ἐκεῖνος μέ τά μαῦρα μαλλιά, My uncle is that one with the black hair.
Ἔχω πολλά λεφτά, I have a lot of money.
Τό κορίτσι μέ τά γκρίζα μάτια, The girl with the grey eyes.
Εἶναι ὅλοι στή βεράντα, They are all on the veranda.
Ἔχω μιάν ἀδελφή καί ἕναν ἀδελφό, I have a sister and a brother.
Ὁ Χρῖστος εἶναι στό σαλόνι, Christos is in the living room.
Πῆγε στό γραφεῖο μ' ἕνα μπουκάλι κρασί, He went to the office with a bottle of wine.
Αὐτά τά τσιγάρα εἶναι γιά τό Γιῶργο, These cigarettes are for George.

EXERCISE 10

Translate:

1. *Θέλω λίγο νερό.*
2. *Εἶναι στήν Κύπρο.*
3. *Τό αὐτοκίνητο εἶναι στό γκαράζ.*
4. *Ὅλη ἡ οἰκογένεια εἶναι στό σπίτι.*
5. *Δέν ἔχω λεφτά.*
6. *Ἔχω μιά χαρά μέσα στήν καρδιά μου.*
7. *Ὁ ἄνθρωπος μέ τό ψηλό καπέλλο εἶναι στή βεράντα.*
8. *Ἐκείνη ἡ γυναίκα μέ τά γκρίζα μαλλιά εἶναι ἡ μητέρα μου.*
9. *Ὁ ἀδελφός μου πῆγε στήν Ἀγγλία καί ἡ ἀδελφή μου στήν Ἑλλάδα.*
10. *Τό δωμάτιό μου εἶναι πάνω ἀπό τό δικό σου.*
11. *Ἦταν στό γραφεῖο του γιά κάμποση ὥρα.*
12. *Τό σπίτι μας εἶναι κοντά στή θάλασσα.*
13. *Τά πόδια του εἶναι μέσα στό νερό.*

14. *Θέλω ἕνα ποτήρι κρασί.*
15. *Ὁ θεῖος μου ἦρθε ἀπό τήν Ἀμερική.*
16. *Εἶδα τό φίλο σου τό Γιάννη στήν Ἀθήνα.*
17. *Αὐτό τό καπέλλο εἶναι γιά τόν Κώστα.*
18. *Δόσε μου ἕνα ποτήρι νερό.*
19. *Δόσε μου τρία μπουκάλια κρασί.*
20. *Ὁ πατέρας μου πῆγε στήν Ἀθήνα γιά δουλειά.*

ACCUSATIVE PLURAL

The accusative plural is formed by changing:

1. M. The plural article *οἱ* into *τούς*.
   F. „ „ „ *οἱ* into *τίς*.
   N. „ „ „ *τά* into *τά*.
2. M. The nominative plural ending *-οι* into *-ους*, e.g. *οἱ φίλοι*, acc. *τούς φίλους*.

All other endings remain the same as in the nominative plural.

EXAMPLES

Ἔχω δυό ἀδελφές καί τρεῖς ἀδελφούς, I have two sisters and three brothers.

Δόσε μου δέκα τσιγάρα, παρακαλῶ, Give me ten cigarettes, please.

Στό πάρτυ τοῦ Γιάννη εἶδα πολλούς ἄντρες ἀλλά λίγες γυναῖκες, At John's party I saw many men but few women.

VOCABULARY

τό σπίρτο, match
τό τραπέζι, table
τό τηλέφωνο, telephone
ἡ κουζίνα, kitchen
ἡ Γαλλία, France
τό παλτό, overcoat
εἶδα, I saw
ἔχει, has (he, she, it)
τό κουτί, box
παρακαλῶ, please
τώρα, now
ποῦ; where?
τό Λονδῖνο, London
ἡ Θεσσαλονίκη, Salonica
ὁ δρόμος, street
ἡ εἴσοδος,* entrance
τό σινεμά, cinema

* Some F nouns end in *-ος*, e.g. *ἡ νῆσος*, island, which is declined as follows: Sing.: nom. *ἡ νῆσος*, gen. *τῆς νήσου*, acc. *τή νῆσο*. Plur.: nom. *αἱ νῆσοι*, gen. *τῶν νήσων*, acc. *τάς νήσους*.

EXERCISE 11

Translate:

1. *Εἶδα τόν ἀδελφό σου στό δρόμο.*
2. *Τό νερό εἶναι πάνω στό τραπέζι.*
3. *Ἡ ἀδελφή μου εἶναι στή Γαλλία.*
4. *Τό αὐτοκίνητο τοῦ πατέρα μου εἶναι κοντά στήν εἴσοδο τοῦ σινεμᾶ.*
5. *Ὁ θεῖος μου ἔχει πολλά λεφτά.*
6. *Ὁ μικρός μου ἀδελφός εἶναι μόνο πέντε χρονῶν.*
7. *Ἐκεῖνος ὁ ἄνθρωπος μέ τά γκρίζα μαλλιά εἶναι ὁ πατέρας μου.*
8. *Ποῦ εἶναι ὁ Ἀντρέας; Εἶναι στό σινεμά.*
9. *Ποῦ εἶναι ὁ ἀδελφός σου; Πῆγε στή θάλασσα μέ τούς φίλους του.*
10. *Τό φῶς αὐτοῦ τοῦ δωματίου δέν εἶναι δυνατό.*
11. *Ποῦ εἶναι τώρα ὁ Κώστας; Εἶναι στό γραφεῖο του.*
12. *Ποῦ εἶναι τό παλτό μου; Εἶναι στό σαλόνι.*
13. *Δόσε μου λίγο κρασί, παρακαλῶ.*
14. *Τώρα δέν ἔχω λεφτά.*

EXERCISE 12

1. My father is in London.
2. The children are by the sea.
3. The wine is in the bottle.
4. The bottle is on the table.
5. I have one brother and one sister.
6. George went to Salonica.
7. Your friend is on the veranda.
8. The telephone is in the living room.
9. Where is my breakfast?
10. The breakfast is in the kitchen.
11. Where are the children?

12. The children are in the garden.
13. That tall man is my uncle.
14. He went to England by plane.
15. He went with my brother.
16. My mother is not at home now.
17. All the family went to the sea.
18. I have not much money.
19. I want some water.
20. My brother is at his work, now.
21. The telephone is not by the door.
22. The boy is under the table.
23. This wine is for your father.
24. Give me some water, please.
25. Give me ten cigarettes and a box of matches.

TELLING THE TIME

VOCABULARY

τί, what
τό τέταρτο, quarter
μισός, half
δώδεκα, twelve
δεκατρεῖς, δεκατρία, thirteen
δεκατέσσερεις, -α, fourteen
δεκαπέντε, fifteen
τριάντα, thirty
πενήντα, fifty
ἑβδομήντα, seventy
ἐνενήντα, ninety
τό λεπτό, minute
παρά, minus
ἕντεκα, eleven
εἴκοσι, twenty
εἰκοσιδύο, twenty-two
εἰκοσιπέντε, twenty-five
σαράντα, forty
ἑξήντα, sixty
ὀγδόντα, eighty
ἑκατό, hundred

The thing to note about telling the time is that the hour is put first followed by *καί*, plus, or *παρά*, minus, and the appropriate fraction or number of minutes, e.g.

Τί ὥρα εἶναι; What time is it?
Εἶναι τρεῖς, It is three.
or *Εἶναι ἡ ὥρα τρεῖς*, It is three o'clock.
Εἶναι ἡ ὥρα μία, It is one o'clock.

Note that the numerals *μία, τρεῖς*, etc., and the adjective *μισή* are in concord with *ὥρα* which is a class F noun. The N forms *τρία*, etc., are used when they refer to N class nouns such as *λεπτά*, e.g.

Εἶναι ἡ ὥρα τρεῖς καί τρία λεπτά, It is three minutes past three.
Τί ὥρα εἶναι παρακαλῶ; What is the time, please?

Τώρα εἶναι τρεῖς καί τέταρτο, Now it is a quarter past three.
Ὄχι, δέν εἶναι τρεῖς καί τέταρτο, εἶναι τρεῖς παρά τέταρτο, No, it is not quarter past three, it is quarter to three.
Τώρα εἶναι πέντε καί μισή, Now it is half past five.
Τώρα εἶναι ἑφτά μιση, Now it is half past seven.

The *καί* in front of the *μισή* is sometimes omitted, in which case the accent is always removed to the last syllable of the numerals, e.g.

Εἶναι πεντέ μιση, It is half past five.

In the case of *τρεῖς* and *τέσσερεις* an *ή* sound is added in front of the *μιση* and the accent falls on this *η*, e.g.

Εἶναι τρεῖς ἥμιση, It is half past three.

Εἶναι δώδεκα παρά πέντε λεπτά, It is five to twelve.
Εἶναι ἕντεκα καί πέντε, It is five past eleven.
Ὁ Γιάννης ἦρθε στίς πέντε, John came at five.
Μιά ὥρα ἔχει ἑξήντα λεπτά, An hour has sixty minutes.
Ἑκατό λεπτά εἶναι μιά ὥρα καί σαράντα λεπτά, A hundred minutes is one hour and forty minutes.

EXERCISE 13

Write in full:

1. 3.15′. 2. 12.0′. 3. 8.50′. 4. 6.45′. 5. 4.5′. 6. 9.10′. 7. 7.30. 8. 10.30. 9. 1.0. 10. 3.45. 11. 1.4′. 12. 80 λεπτά εἶναι μιά ὥρα καί 20 λεπτά. 13. 90 λεπτά εἶναι μιά ὥρα καί 30 λεπτά. 14. 65 λεπτά εἶναι μιά ὥρα καί 5 λεπτά.

VOCABULARY

ἡ *Κυριακή*, Sunday
ἡ *Δευτέρα*, Monday
ἡ *Τρίτη*, Tuesday
ἡ *Τετάρτη*, Wednesday
ἡ *Πέμπτη*, Thursday
ἡ *Παρασκευή*, Friday
τό *Σάββατο*, Saturday
τελευταῖος, last
ἡ *τάξη*, class
ὁ *μαθητής*, student, pupil
δέκατος, tenth
εἰκοστός, twentieth
ἴσος, equal
ἡ *μέρα*, day
ἡ *ἑβδομάδα*, week
πρῶτος, first
δεύτερος, second
τρίτος, third
τέταρτος, fourth
πέμπτος, fifth
ἕκτος, sixth
ἕβδομος, seventh
ὄγδοος, eighth
ἔνατος, ninth
ἑκατοστός, hundredth
δέκατος τρίτος, thirteentn

EXAMPLES

Ἡ Κυριακή εἶναι ἡ πρώτη μέρα τῆς ἑβδομάδας, Sunday is the first day of the week.
Ὁ Βάσος εἶναι ὁ ἕκτος μαθητής στήν τάξη του, Vassos is the sixth pupil in his class.
Ἕνα δέκατο εἶναι ἴσο μέ δέκα ἑκατοστά, One tenth is equal to ten hundredths.

EXERCISE 14

Translate:

1. *Τό Σάββατο εἶναι ἡ τελευταία μέρα τῆς ἑβδομάδας.*
2. *Ὁ Κώστας πῆγε στή θάλασσα τήν Τετάρτη.*
3. *Ἡ Κυριακή εἶναι μιά εὐχάριστη μέρα.*
4. *Μιά ἑβδομάδα ἔχει ἑφτά μέρες.*
5. *Ὁ Ρένος εἶναι ὁ δεύτερος μαθητής στήν τάξη του.*
6. *Πέντε ἑκατοστά εἶναι ἴσα μέ ἕνα εἰκοστό.*
7. *Ἕνα δέκατο τρίτο εἶναι ἴσο μέ δύο εἰκοστά ἕκτα.*
8. *Μισή ὥρα εἶναι ἴση μέ τριάντα λεπτά.*

COMPARISON OF ADJECTIVES

Adjectives form their comparative mostly by taking the word *πιό* (= more) in front of them. They are then followed by the preposition *ἀπό* and the accusative, e.g.

Ὁ Μιχάλης εἶναι πλούσιος, Michael is rich.
Ὁ Μιχάλης εἶναι πιό πλούσιος ἀπό τόν Κώστα, Michael is richer than Costas.

Another way of forming the comparative, usual with shorter words, is by changing the endings as follows:

M. *-ος* into *-ότερος*
F. *-η* or *-α* into *-ότερη*
N. *-ο* into *-ότερο*

e.g.		
δυνατός	*δυνατότερος*	stronger
μικρός	*μικρότερος*	smaller
ὡραῖος	*ὡραιότερος*	more beautiful
εὔκολος	*εὐκολότερος*	easier

A few adjectives form their comparative by changing the endings,

M. *-ος* into *-ύτερος*
F. *-η* or *-α* into *-ύτερη*
N. *-ο* into *-ύτερο*

e.g.		
καλός	*καλύτερος*	better
μεγάλος	*μεγαλύτερος*	bigger, greater, older

The comparative of *κακός*, bad, is *χειρότερος*, worse.

EXAMPLES

Ὁ ἀδελφός μου εἶναι πιό δυνατός ἀπό τόν ἀδελφό σου, My brother is stronger than your brother.

Ὁ Γιάννης εἶναι φτωχότερος ἀπό τόν Κώστα, John is poorer than Costas.

*Αὐτό τό σπίτι εἶναι καλύτερο ἀπ' ἐκεῖνο,** This house is better than that one.

Αὐτό τό αὐτοκίνητο εἶναι πολύ χειρότερο ἀπό τό ἄλλο, This car is much worse than the other one.

The superlative

The superlative is formed by putting the definite article in front of the comparative. The superlative is followed by either the preposition *σέ* (*σ'*) or the genitive case, e.g.

Ὁ Ἀντρέας εἶναι ὁ καλύτερος μαθητής στήν τάξη του, Andrew is the best pupil in his class.

Ὁ πατέρας της εἶναι ὁ πιό πλούσιος τῆς Ἀθήνας, Her father is the richest man in Athens.

Ἡ Ἑλένη ἦταν ἡ ὡραιότερη γυναίκα τῆς Ἑλλάδας, Helen was the most beautiful woman in Greece.

Some adjectives change the endings,

M. -*ος* into -*ότατος*
F. -*η* or -*α* into -*ότατη*
N. -*ο* into -*ότατο*

to express a superlative degree, e.g.

Τό πάρτυ του ἦταν λαμπρότατο, His party was most wonderful.

* The final -*ο* of *ἀπό* may be replaced by an apostrophe in front of a vowel.

EXERCISE 15

Translate:

1. *Τό σπίτι σας εἶναι μικρότερο ἀπό τό δικό μας.*
2. *Ὁ Γιάννης εἶναι μεγαλύτερος ἀπό τόν Πέτρο.*
3. *Αὐτό εἶναι τό καλύτερο ἀπ' ὅλα.*
4. *Ὁ Πλάτων ἦταν ὁ μεγαλύτερος φιλόσοφος τῆς Ἑλλάδας.*
5. *Αὐτή ἡ δουλειά εἶναι δυσκολότατη.*
6. *Αὐτό τό κρασί εἶναι πιό δυνατό ἀπ' ἐκεῖνο.*
7. *Ἡ Μύκονος εἶναι ὡραιότερη ἀλλά πολύ πιό ζεστή ἀπό τήν Καβάλλα.*
8. *Ἡ Ἀγγλία εἶναι μεγαλύτερη ἀπό τήν Ἰρλανδία.*

SUMMARY OF PRINCIPAL FORMS OF NOUNS

	M	F	N
		Singular	
Nom.	*ὅ κῆπος*	*ἥ φωνή*	*τό γραφεῖο*
Gen.	*τοῦ κήποι*	*τῆς φωνῆς*	*τοῦ γραφείου*
Acc.	*τόν κῆπο*	*τή φωνή*	*τό γραφεῖο*
		Plural	
Nom.	*οἵ κῆποι*	*οἵ φωνές*	*τά γραφεῖα*
Gen.	*τῶν κήπων*	*τῶν φωνῶν*	*τῶν γραφείων*
Acc.	*τούς κήπους*	*τίς φωνές*	*τά γραφεῖα*
		Singular	
Nom.	*ὅ ἐργάτης*	*ἥ καρδιά*	*τό παιδί*
Gen.	*τοῦ ἐργάτη*	*τῆς καρδιᾶς*	*τοῦ παιδιοῦ*
Acc.	*τόν ἐργάτη*	*τήν καρδιά*	*τό παιδί*
		Plural	
Nom.	*οἵ ἐργάτες*	*οἵ καρδιές*	*τά παιδιά*
Gen.	*τῶν ἐργατῶν*	*τῶν καρδιῶν*	*τῶν παιδιῶν*
Acc.	*τούς ἐργάτες*	*τίς καρδιές*	*τά παιδιά*

VERBS

Verbs change to express person, number and time. They are divided into two general classes which may be termed Active and Passive.

Active are those ending in *-ω* in the first person singular of the present tense,* e.g. *ἔχω*, I have; *θέλω*, I want. These verbs are usually called Active because they mostly denote an action done by the subject.

Passive are those ending in *-μαι* in the first person singular of the present tense, e.g. *διδάσκομαι*, I am taught; *φοβᾶμαι*, I am afraid. These verbs are usually called Passive because they mostly denote an action suffered by the subject.

This last distinction is not, however, rigid. Thus *ἔρχομαι*, I come, has a Passive ending while it denotes an action done by the subject.

In other cases what a Greek would consider as a Passive verb is not so considered by an English person, e.g. *θυμᾶμαι*, I remember; *στέκομαι*, I stand.

ACTIVE VERBS

Most verbs belong to the Active class. These are divided into two further classes determined by the position of the accent.

I. Verbs not accented on the last syllable, e.g. *ἔχω*, I have; *θέλω*, I want; *κλείω*, I close.

II. Verbs accented on the last syllable, e.g. *μπορῶ*, I can; *ἀπαντῶ*, I answer.

* We shall be considering the form of the first person singular as the basic form of the verb.

I. Most verbs belong to the first class. They are divided into the following sub-classes according to the way they change the ending of the first person singular of the present tense to form the first person singular of the Indefinite tense.*

I*a*. Verbs changing the ending -*ω*, -*ζω* or -*νω*, and -*φτω* into -*σω*, e.g. Pres. *κλείω*, I close; Indef. *κλείσω*. Pres. *ἀρχίζω*, I begin; Indef. *ἀρχίσω*. Pres. *πιάνω*, I take; Indef. *πιάσω*. Pres. *πέφτω*, I fall; Indef. *πέσω*.

I*b*. Verbs changing the ending -*βω*, -*υω* (pronounced *vo*) or -*πω* into -*ψω*, e.g. Pres. *κόβω*, I cut; Indef. *κόψω*. Pres. *δουλεύω*, I work; Indef. *δουλέψω*. Pres. *λείπω*, I am away; Indef. *λείψω*.

I*c*. Verbs changing the ending -*ζω*, -*χνω*, -*χω* and -*γω* into -*ξω*, e.g. Pres. *ἀλλάζω*, I change; Indef. *ἀλλάξω*. Pres. *δείχνω*, I show; Indef. *δείξω*. Pres. *προσέχω*, I notice; Indef. *προσέξω*. Pres. *ἀνοίγω*, I open; Indef. *ἀνοίξω*.

I*d*. Verbs that do not change anything, e.g. Pres. *κάνω*, I do, make; Indef. *κάνω*. Pres. *ξέρω*, I know; Indef. *ξέρω*. Pres. *φέρω*, I bring; Indef. *φέρω*.

I*e*. Verbs undergoing several irregular changes. These irregular forms must be learned individually, as no simple rule can be given for their formation. In some cases the Indefinite form is completely different from that of the Present. These irregular verbs should be given thorough attention as most of them are very frequent words, e.g. Pres. *λέγω*, I say; Indef. *πῶ*. Pres. *βλέπω*, I see; Indef. *δῶ*. Pres. *δίνω*, I give; Indef. *δόσω*. Pres. *πηγαίνω*, I go; Indef. *πάω*.

II. Some verbs belong to the second class, i.e. they are accented on the last syllable. They are divided into the

* The Indefinite is roughly equivalent to the English Infinitive, e.g. I want to *go* (*Θέλω νά πάω*), and does not usually stand by itself. For its use see pages 67, 88, 145.

following sub-classes according to the way they change the final -*ῶ* of the first person singular of the Present to form the first person singular of the Indefinite.

II*a*. Verbs changing -*ῶ* into -*ήσω*, e.g. Pres. *ἀπαντῶ*, I answer; Indef. *ἀπαντήσω*. *τραβῶ*, I pull, becomes *τραβήξω** in the Indefinite. The great majority of verbs of the second class belong to this sub-class.

II*b*. Verbs changing -*ῶ* into -*άσω*, e.g. Pres. *γελῶ*, I laugh; Indef. *γελάσω*.

Note that *κοιτῶ*, I look, becomes *κοιτάξω* in the Indefinite.

II*c*. Verbs changing -*ῶ* into -*έσω*, e.g. *μπορῶ*, I can; Indef. *μπορέσω*. This is the only common verb belonging to this sub-class.

II*d*. Irregular verbs, e.g. *περνῶ*, I pass; Indef. *περάσω*.

PRESENT AND FUTURE

The Present tense which has been considered as the basic form of the verb is equivalent to the English Present tense as well as to the Present Continuous, e.g. *κλείνω*, I close, or I am closing; *δουλεύω*, I work, or I am working; *βλέπω*, I see, or I am seeing.

To express an action that will take place in the future the particle *θά* is put in front of the Indefinite. In fact the Indefinite is hardly ever used by itself and cannot properly be translated as such; e.g. *θά κλείσω*, I shall close; *θά δῶ*, I shall see.

A Future Continuous event is expressed by putting *θά* in front of the Present form, e.g. *θά κλείω*, I shall be closing; *θά δουλεύω*, I shall be working; *θά βλέπω*, I shall be seeing.

* *ξ* and *ψ* are a shorter way of writing *κσ* and *πσ* respectively.

FORMATION OF THE INDEFINITE

Below are given the first person singular of the Present and Indefinite forms of the most common verbs in their various sub-classes.

	Present	*Indefinite*
I*a*.	ἀκούω, I hear	ἀκούσω
	κλείω, I close	κλείσω
	ἀρχίζω, I begin	ἀρχίσω
	ἀποφασίζω, I decide	ἀποφασίσω
	γυρίζω, I turn	γυρίσω
	γνωρίζω, I know	γνωρίσω
	γεμίζω, I fill	γεμίσω
	ἐξετάζω, I examine	ἐξετάσω
	μοιάζω, I resemble	μοιάσω
	νομίζω, I think	νομίσω
	συνεχίζω, I continue	συνεχίσω
	φροντίζω, I care for	φροντίσω
	ἀφίνω, I leave	ἀφίσω
	ἁπλώνω, I spread	ἁπλώσω
	πιάνω, I take	πιάσω
	σηκώνω, I lift	σηκώσω
	φτάνω, I reach	φτάσω
	χάνω, I lose	χάσω
	πέφτω, I fall	πέσω
I*b*.	ἀνάβω, I light	ἀνάψω
	κόβω, I cut	κόψω
	κρύβω, I hide	κρύψω
	δουλεύω, I work	δουλέψω
	μαζεύω, I collect	μαζέψω
	χορεύω, I dance	χορέψω
	λείπω, I am absent, away	λείψω

	Present	*Indefinite*
I*c*.	*κοιτάζω*, I look (at)	*κοιτάξω*
	ἀλλάζω, I change	*ἀλλάξω*
	δείχνω, I show	*δείξω*
	ἀνοίγω, I open	*ἀνοίξω*
	προσέχω, I pay attention	*προσέξω*
	ὑπάρχω, I exist	*ὑπάρξω*
	ρίχνω, I throw	*ρίξω*
	ψάχνω, I search	*ψάξω*
I*d*.	*ἔχω*, I have	*ἔχω*
	θέλω, I want	*θέλω*
	κάνω, I do, make	*κάνω*
	ξέρω, I know	*ξέρω*
	φέρω, I bring, fetch	*φέρω*
	ἀνήκω, I belong	*ἀνήκω*
	προτείνω, I suggest	*προτείνω*
	ἀρέσω, I please, I am pleasing to	*ἀρέσω*
I*e*.	*βλέπω*, I see	*δῶ*
	βρίσκω, I find	*βρῶ*
	λέγω, I say	*πῶ*
	δίνω, I give	*δόσω*
	πηγαίνω, I go	*πάω*
	παίρνω, I take	*πάρω*
	πίνω, I drink	*πιῶ*
	βάζω, I put	*βάλω*
	τρώγω, I eat	*φάω*
	μπαίνω, I get in, go in	*μπῶ*
	μένω, I stay	*μείνω*
	φεύγω, I leave	*φύγω*
	καταλαβαίνω, I understand	*καταλάβω*
	βγαίνω, I go out	*βγῶ*
	ἀνεβαίνω, I go up	*ἀνεβῶ*
	κατεβαίνω, I go down	*κατεβῶ*

	Present	*Indefinite*
IIa.	*ἀπαντῶ*, I answer	*ἀπαντήσω*
	ἀποχτῶ, I obtain	*ἀποχτήσω*
	ἀγαπῶ, I love	*ἀγαπήσω*
	ζῶ, I live	*ζήσω*
	ζητῶ, I seek	*ζητήσω*
	θαρρῶ, I think	*θαρρήσω*
	κουνῶ, I move	*κουνήσω*
	κρατῶ, I hold	*κρατήσω*
	μιλῶ, I talk	*μιλήσω*
	ξυπνῶ, I wake	*ξυπνήσω*
	παρατῶ, I abandon	*παρατήσω*
	παρακολουθῶ, I follow, attend	*παρακολουθήσω*
	προχωρῶ, I proceed	*προχωρήσω*
	προσπαθῶ, I try	*προσπαθήσω*
	ρωτῶ, I ask	*ρωτήσω*
	σταματῶ, I stop	*σταματήσω*
	συμφωνῶ, I agree	*συμφωνήσω*
	φιλῶ, I kiss	*φιλήσω*
IIb.	*γελῶ*, I laugh	*γελάσω*
	χαμογελῶ, I smile	*χαμογελάσω*
	χαλῶ, I demolish, spoil	*χαλάσω*
	κοιτῶ, I look (at)	*κοιτάξω*
IIc.	*μπορῶ*, I can	*μπορέσω*
IId.	*περνῶ*, I pass	*περάσω*

EXERCISE 16

Form the first person singular of the Indefinite of the following verbs:

1. *γυρίζω* 2. *προσέχω* 3. *σταματῶ* 4. *ἀνάβω* 5. *θαρρῶ* 6. *μπορῶ* 7. *μοιάζω* 8. *παρακολουθῶ* 9. *ζητῶ* 10. *πιάνω* 11. *κρύβω* 12. *χαμογελῶ* 13. *φτάνω* 14. *προχωρῶ*

15. ξυπνῶ 16. κόβω 17. γεμίζω 18. προσπαθῶ
19. ξέρω 20. ζῶ 21. ρωτῶ 22. ἔχω 23. νομίζω
24. μιλῶ 25. δουλεύω 26. δείχνω 27. προτείνω
28. φεύγω 29. πίνω 30. καταλαβαίνω 31. λέγω
32. περνῶ 33. βλέπω 34. δίνω 35. μένω.

EXERCISE 17

Which is the present form of the following Indefinite forms:

1. δείξω 2. φέρω 3. κρύψω 4. συνεχίσω 5. χορέψω
6. ἀπαντήσω 7. φάγω 8. πῶ 9. κουνήσω
10. γελάσω 11. ζητήσω 12. φροντίσω 13. προχωρήσω 14. κοιτάξω 15. μπορέσω 16. ἔχω
17. φτάσω 18. κάνω 19. ἐξετάσω 20. κλείσω
21. κρατήσω 22. χαλάσω 23. προσπαθήσω 24. βάλω
25. καταλάβω 26. δῶ.

VOCABULARY

κλείω, I close
ἀρχίζω, I start
τά χρήματα, money
παρακολουθῶ, I attend
τό μάθημα, lesson
ἡ μηχανική, engineering
κάθε, every
τό πιάνο, piano
βλέπω, I see
θέλω, I want
γνωρίζω, I know
τρώγω, I eat
πίνω, I drink
ἡ μπύρα, beer
ἡ λίρα, pound

EXAMPLES

Κλείω τήν πόρτα, I close (I am closing) the door.
'Αρχίζω δουλειά στίς ὀκτώ τό πρωΐ, I start work at eight in the morning.

Δέν ἔχω χρήματα, I haven't got any money.
Παρακολουθῶ μαθήματα μηχανικῆς, I attend engineering lessons.
Θέλω δέκα τσιγάρα, I want ten cigarettes.

EXERCISE 18

Translate:

1. *Πηγαίνω στή δουλειά μέ αὐτοκίνητο.*
2. *Ἔχω μόνο τρεῖς λίρες.*
3. *Παρακολουθῶ μαθήματα πιάνου.*
4. *Βλέπω ἕνα ἀεροπλάνο.*
5. *Θέλω λίγο νερό.*
6. *Ἔχω ἕναν ἀδελφό καί δύο ἀδελφές.*
7. *Γνωρίζω τό θεῖο σας.*
8. *Τώρα τρώγω.*

VOCABULARY

πηγαίνω, I go
λέγω, I say
δουλεύω, I work
ἡ ἀλήθεια, truth
τό φίλμ, film
αὔριο, tomorrow
μιλῶ, I talk, I speak
τό θάρρος, courage
τό ἀρνάκι, lamb
ἡ χώρα, country
τό θαῦμα, miracle
ἡ Ἀλίκη, Alice
γυρίζω, I turn, return
ἡ Ἀνατολή, East
ὁλάκερος, whole
ἀπαντῶ, I answer
ἐρώτησις, question
ξυπνῶ, I wake up
διαβάζω, I read
ὥς, till
τό ἀπόγευμα, afternoon
τό κρασί, wine

EXAMPLES

Θά πάω στήν Ἀθήνα, I shall go to Athens.
Θά πῶ τήν ἀλήθεια, I will tell the truth.

Θά πιῶ κρασί, I will drink wine.
Θά δῶ ἕνα καλό φίλμ; I shall see a good film.
Αὔριο θά δουλεύω ὅλη μέρα, Tomorrow I shall be working all day.

EXERCISE 19

Translate:

1. *Θά μιλήσω μέ θάρρος.*
2. *Θά πάω στήν 'Αμερική.*
3. *Τό Σάββατο θά πάω στή θάλασσα.*
4. *Θά φάω ἀρνάκι ψητό.*
5. *Θά πάω στό σινεμά καί θά δῶ τήν 'Αλίκη στή Χώρα τῶν Θαυμάτων.*
6. *Θά γυρίσω τήν 'Ανατολή ὁλάκερη.*
7. *Θά ἀπαντήσω στήν ἐρώτησή σου.*
8. *Αὔριο θά ξυπνήσω στίς ἑπτά τό πρωΐ.*
9. *Αὔριο θά διαβάζω ἀπό τίς τρεῖς ὡς τίς ἕξι τό ἀπόγευμα.*

PERSON AND NUMBER

Verbs change to denote person and number. They change their ending to show whether the person to which they refer is the speaker (first person) or the listener (second person) or anyone else (third person), and also whether it is one person (singular number) or more than one person (plural number).

The change in the ending of the verb affords a sufficient distinction of person and number and so the personal pronouns corresponding to the English I, you, he, etc. are usually omitted.

Up to now only the form of the first person singular has been examined. This form can be considered as the basic form of the verb from which we can derive all the other forms in the following way.

The second person (of the) singular (number) of both the Present and the Indef. is formed:*

1. by changing the final *-ω* of class I verbs into *-εις*, e.g. *κλείνω*, I close; *κλείνεις*, you close; *θέλω*, I want; *θέλεις*, you want; *ἀνάψω–ἀνάψεις; ρωτήσω–ρωτήσεις*.
2. by changing the final *-ῶ* of class II verbs into *-ᾶς*, e.g. *ἀπαντῶ*, I answer; *ἀπαντᾶς*, you answer; *ξυπνῶ*, I awake; *ξυπνᾶς*, you awake.

Some of these verbs, however, change into *-εῖς*, e.g. *ζῶ*, I live; *ζεῖς*, you live; *μπορῶ*, I can; *μπορεῖς*, you can. Such verbs are also, *θαρρῶ*, *προσπαθῶ*, etc. Some verbs, like *ζητῶ*, *συμφωνῶ*, etc., change into either *-ᾶς* or *-εῖς*.

* The second person of the singular corresponds to the old English *thou*, but it is commonly used when speaking informally or familiarly.

The third person singular is formed by omitting the final -*ς* of the second person, e.g. *κλείνει*, he (she, it) closes; *θέλει*, he (she, it) wants; *άπαντᾶ*, he (she, it) answers; *ζεῖ*, he (she, it) lives; *ἀνάψει*, etc. The first person plural is formed by changing the final -*ω* of the first person singular into -*ουμε*, e.g. *κλείνω*, I close; *κλείνουμε*, we close; *θέλω*, I want; *θέλουμε*, we want; *ἀπαντῶ*, I answer; *ἀπαντοῦμε*, we answer; *ἀγαπῶ*, I love; *ἀγαποῦμε*, we love; *ἀνάψω*–*ἀνάψουμε*.

Many of those verbs which form the second person singular with -*ᾶς* form the first person plural with -*ᾶμε*, e.g. *μιλᾶς*, you talk; *μιλᾶμε*, we talk; *ξυπνᾶς*, you wake up; *ξυπνᾶμε*, we wake up; *ἀγαπᾶμε*, we love.

The second person plural is formed by changing the ending of the second person singular as follows:

-*εις*	into -*ετε*, e.g. *κλείνεις*, you close (sing.); *κλείνετε*, you close.
-*ᾶς*	into -*ᾶτε*, e.g. *ρωτᾶς*, you ask; *ρωτᾶτε*, you ask.
-*εῖς* (accented)	into *εῖτε*, e.g. *μπορεῖς*, you can; *μπορεῖτε*, you can; *δεῖς*–*δεῖτε*.

The third person plural is formed by changing the *ει* of the third person singular into -*ουν* and -*α* into -*ᾶν* or -*οῦν*, e.g. *ἔχω*, I have; *ἔχουν*, they have; *κουνῶ*, I move, *κουνᾶν*, they move; *ζῶ*, I live; *ζοῦν*, they live; *δόσω*–*δόσουν*. A final -*ε* may be added to these forms, e.g. *ἔχουνε*, they have; *ζοῦνε*, they live, etc.

FORMS OF THE PRESENT

I	II
ἔχω, I have	*γελῶ*, I laugh
ἔχεις, you have	*γελᾶς*, you laugh
ἔχει, he has	*γελᾶ*, he laughs
ἔχουμε, we have	*γελᾶμε*, we laugh
ἔχετε, you have	*γελᾶτε*, you laugh
ἔχουν, they have	*γελοῦν*, they laugh

IIc

μπορῶ, I can
μπορεῖς, you can
μπορεῖ, he can
μποροῦμε, we can
μπορεῖτε, you can
μποροῦν, they can

VOCABULARY

τό τσάϊ, tea
ὁ καφές, coffee
ἀπόψε, tonight
τό θέατρο, theatre
γελῶ, I laugh
τό ζήτημα, question, problem
τό παράθυρο, window
ἡ πόλις, town
πολλοί, a lot, many
ἡ κρεββατοκάμαρα, bedroom
τό ραδιόφωνο, radio
ρωτῶ, enquire
τό φθινόπωρο, autumn
ἡ Ἀγγλική, English language
ὁ ὁρίζοντας, horizon
ἡ ἡσυχία, quiet
ἡ Γερμανία, Germany
ἡ μουσική, music
ἡ βάρκα, boat
μένω, I stay
τό ξενοδοχεῖο, hotel
καταλαβαίνω,. understand
παρακαλῶ, please
τίποτε, nothing, anything
εὐχαριστῶ, thanks!
καπνίζω, I smoke
γιατί, why

EXAMPLES

1. *Πίνω τσάϊ*, I drink tea.
2. *Πίνετε τσάϊ ἤ καφέ;* Do you drink tea or coffee?
3. *᾿Απόψε θά πᾶμε στό θέατρο*, Tonight we shall go to the theatre.
4. *Μή γελᾶτε. Τό ζήτημα εἶναι σοβαρό*, Don't laugh, the matter is serious.
5. *Τά παιδιά διαβάζουν στήν κρεββατοκάμαρα*, The children read (or are reading) in the bedroom.
6. *῾Ο Γιάννης θά μιλήσει ἀπό τό ραδιόφωνο*, John will speak on the radio.
7. *῎Εχεις ἕνα τσιγάρο;* Have you got a cigarette?
8. *Γιατί ρωτᾶς;* Why do you ask?

EXERCISE 20

Translate:

1. *Τό φθινόπωρο θά παρακολουθήσω μαθήματα ᾿Αγγλικῆς*
2. *Βλέπετε ἐκεῖνο τό ἀεροπλάνο στόν ὁρίζοντα;*
3. *῎Εχουμε λεφτά ἀλλά δέν ἔχουμε ἡσυχία.*
4. *Θέλετε λίγο νερό;*
5. *῾Ο πατέρας θά πάει στή Γερμανία.*
6. *Ποῦ μένετε;*
7. *Μένω στό ξενοδοχεῖο ᾿Αστόρια.*
8. *Γνωρίζετε τό θεῖο μου; Ναί, ἀλλά δέν εἶναι φίλος μου.*
9. *Δέν καταλαβαίνω.*
10. *Τί θέλετε, παρακαλῶ;*
11. *Τίποτε, εὐχαριστῶ.*
12. *Καπνίζω δέκα τσιγάρα τήν ἡμέρα.*
13. *Γιατί γελᾶτε παρακαλῶ;*

EXERCISE 21

Translate:

1. I am closing the window.
2. We shall go to France.
3. They do not want tea.
4. I work in town.
5. Have you got much money?
6. I have (attend) music lessons.
7. Do you see a boat on the sea?
8. My father does (can) not see very far.
9. We will go to America and John will go to France.
10. Do you smoke?
11. I don't smoke.
12. We don't drink beer.
13. I want a glass of wine.
14. We want a house by the sea.
15. Tomorrow we shall go to Mykonos.
16. I don't want tea, I want coffee.

THE PAST TENSE

The first person singular of the Past tense is formed from the Indefinite by:

(i) Changing the final *ω* into *-α*.

(ii) Removing the accent to the third syllable from the end, e.g. Pres. *συνεχίζω*, I continue; Indef. *συνεχίσω*; Past *συνέχισα*, I continued. Pres. *δουλεύω*, I work; Indef. *δουλέψω*; Past *δούλεψα*, I worked. Pres. *σταματῶ*; Indef. *σταματήσω*; Past *σταμάτησα*, I stopped. Pres. *ρωτῶ*, I ask; Indef. *ρωτήσω*; Past *ρώτησα*, I asked.

Where there is no third syllable, as in two-syllable words of class I or one-syllable words of class II, an initial *ε-* (called an augment) is added to the Past form, e.g. Pres. *χάνω*, I lose; Indef. *χάσω*; Past *ἔχασα*, I lost. Pres. *ζῶ*, I live; Indef. *ζήσω*; Past *ἔζησα*, I lived.

The verb *ξέρω* takes *η* at the beginning: *ἤξερα*, I knew. Verbs of sub-class I*e* (irregular verbs) form their Past tense in unusual ways which are, however, based on the form of the Indefinite. These forms should be learned individually. Here are the commonest verbs of this sub-class:

Present	*Past*	
βλέπω	*εἶδα*	I saw
βρίσκω	*βρῆκα*	I found
λέγω	*εἶπα*	I said
δίνω	*ἔδοσα*	I gave
πηγαίνω	*πῆγα*	I went
παίρνω	*πῆρα*	I took
πίνω	*ἤπια*	I drank

Present	*Past*	
βάζω	*ἔβαλα*	I put
τρώγω	*ἔφαγα*	I ate
μπαίνω	*μπῆκα*	I entered
μένω	*ἔμεινα*	I stayed
φεύγω	*ἔφυγα*	I left
καταλαβαίνω	*κατάλαβα*	I understood
βγαίνω	*βγῆκα*	I went out
ἀνεβαίνω	*ἀνέβηκα*	I went up
κατεβαίνω	*κατέβηκα*	I went down
ἔχω	*εἶχα*	I had

The other persons of the Past tense are formed by changing the final *-α* of the first person singular as follows:

Singular

Second person into	*-ες*
Third person into	*-ε*

Plural

First person into	*-αμε*
Second person into	*-ατε*
Third person into	*-αν(ε).*

e.g.

γύρισα, I returned	*προχώρησα*, I proceeded
γύρισες, you returned	*προχώρησες*, you proceeded
γύρισε, he returned	*προχώρησε*, he proceeded
γυρίσαμε, we returned	*προχωρήσαμε*, we proceeded
γυρίσατε, you returned	*προχωρήσατε*, you proceeded
γύρισαν, they returned	*προχώρησαν*, they proceeded
or	or
γυρίσανε, they returned	*προχωρήσανε*, they proceeded

Verbs which take the augment *ε-* (a vowel prefixed to the

verb) to form the Past tense usually drop it in the first and second persons plural. These forms can dispense with the augment as they have three syllables, e.g.

ἔχασα, I lost	*ἔφυγα*, I left
ἔχασες, you lost	*ἔφυγες*, you left
ἔχασε, he lost	*ἔφυγε*, he left
χάσαμε, we lost	*φύγαμε*, we left
χάσατε, you lost	*φύγατε*, you left
ἔχασαν, they lost	*ἔφυγαν*, they left
χάσανε, they lost	*φύγανε*, they left

EXERCISE 22

Form the Past tense of these verbs:

1. *γυρίζω* 2. *νομίζω* 3. *μαζεύω* 4. *κόβω* 5. *φέρω* 6. *φτάνω* 7. *ψάχνω* 8. *βλέπω* 9. *κατεβαίνω* 10. *ἀπαντῶ* 11. *πηγαίνω* 12. *κρατῶ* 13. *ρωτῶ* 14. *μπορῶ* 15. *κουνῶ* 16. *σταματῶ* 17. *ζῶ* 18. *προχωρῶ* 19. *τρώγω* 20. *μένω* 21. *χάνω* 22. *ἔχω*.

The Past tense is one of the most frequent tenses in the language. It corresponds to both the English Past tense and the English Perfect. Thus, *Πῆγα στό γιατρό* may mean according to the context, either *I went to the doctor* or *I have been to the doctor*.

VOCABULARY

ὁ ἄλλος, the other (one)	*τό μέσο*, middle
χαμογελῶ, I smile	*πρός*, towards
σιωπηλός, silent	*βγαίνω*, I go out
ἀφίνω, I leave	*κουνῶ*, I move
τό τζάκι, hearth	*συνεχίζω*, I continue
προχωρῶ, I proceed	*ἡ κουβέντα*, talk

διάφορος, different
παίρνω, I take
τό γράμμα, letter
ὁ ἀξιωματικός, officer
φεύγω, I go away
ἡ συγκέντρωση, meeting
τό αἷμα, blood
ἀνεβαίνω, I go up
ξέρω, I know
πολλά, a lot
ὁ χοντρός, fat man
ἀνάβω, light
νωρίς, early
πίσω, back
ἀκούω, I hear
ὁ καιρός, weather
πολύς, much, long (of time)
στέλνω, I send
τό πακέτο, packet
ζῶ, I live
ὁ χρόνος, year
ἡ Νεάπολη, Naples
πάντα, always
χτές, yesterday
τό τραῖνο, train
ἡ Λευκοσία, Nicosia
σταματῶ, I stop
βάζω, I put
ὕστερα, then, later

EXAMPLES

Πῆγε στήν Αἴγυπτο μέ κάμποσα λεφτά, He went to Egypt with a lot of money.
Ὁ ἄλλος χαμογέλασε, The other one smiled.
Γιά κάμποση ὥρα ἔμειναν σιωπηλοί, For a long time they remained silent.
Ὁ Ἀντρέας δέν ἀπάντησε, Andrew did not answer.
Ἔκλεισε τά μάτια του, He closed his eyes.
Ἄφισε τό ποτήρι του στό τζάκι καί προχώρησε πρός τό μέσο τοῦ δωματίου, He left his glass on the mantelpiece and advanced to the middle of the room.
Βγῆκαν κι' οἱ τρεῖς στή βεράντα, They all three went out on to the veranda.

EXERCISE 23

Translate:

1. *Οἱ ἀξιωματικοί ἔφυγαν ἀπό τή συγκέντρωση.*
2. *Τό αἷμα ἀνέβηκε στό κεφάλι του.*
3. *Ὁ ἄνθρωπος αὐτός ἤξερε πολλά.*
4. *Ὁ χοντρός δέν ἀπάντησε.*
5. *Ἔστειλα ἕνα πακέτο στή μητέρα μου.*
6. *Ἔζησαν τρία χρόνια στή Νεάπολη.*
7. *Ὁ πατέρας μου εἶχε πάντα λεφτά.*
8. *Χτές εἶδα τό Γιῶργο στό τραίνο.*
9. *Ἡ κυρία Λαμπρίδη κούνησε τό κεφάλι της.*
10. *Στήν πόρτα ἡ Ἔλενα γύρισε πίσω.*
11. *Ἔμεινα στό ξενοδοχεῖο.*
12. *Πῆγε κοντά του καί τοῦ μίλησε.*
13. *Συνέχισαν τήν κουβέντα τους πάνω σέ διάφορα ζητήματα.*
14. *Πῆρα τό γράμμα σου.*
15. *Ἄναψε ἕνα σπίρτο.*
16. *Γύρισε νωρίς στό σπίτι.*

EXERCISE 24

Translate:

1. He went to Italy.
2. We went to Germany.
3. They went to England.
4. You went to France.
5. Did you (sing.) go to America?
6. Did you go to the theatre yesterday?
7. Have you heard?
8. Peter did not understand.
9. They stayed at our house for a long time.
10. I saw your brother in Nicosia.

11. I have read Anna Karenina.
12. He stopped for a while (*λίγο*), he smiled and then said . . .
13. She closed her eyes.
14. Yesterday I woke up very early.
15. They put the car in the garage.
16. He left yesterday morning.

IMPERFECT

The Imperfect tense is formed in the same way as the Past tense but by using as basis the Present instead of the Indefinite. Verbs of class I conform rigidly to this pattern, e.g.

Present	*Imperfect*	
λέγω	ἔλεγα	I was saying
πηγαίνω	πήγαινα	I was going
μένω	ἔμενα	I was staying
καταλαβαίνω	καταλάβαινα	I was understanding
πέφτω	ἔπεφτα	I was falling
ἀνοίγω	ἄνοιγα	I was opening
θέλω	ἤθελα	I wanted

Verbs of class II change the final -ῶ of the Present into -οῦσα (accented) or -αγα* (unaccented) and drop the augment, e.g.

ζητῶ	ζητοῦσα	ζήταγα	I was looking for
μιλῶ	μιλοῦσα	μίλαγα	I was talking
ζῶ	ζοῦσα		I was living
κρατῶ	κρατοῦσα	κράταγα	I was holding
προσπαθῶ	προσπαθοῦσα		I was trying

FORMS OF THE IMPERFECT

ἔλεγα	πήγαινα	κρατοῦσα
ἔλεγες	πήγαινες	κρατοῦσες
ἔλεγε	πήγαινε	κρατοῦσε

* The suffix -αγα is used only in two-syllabled words. It is not so frequent as the other suffix.

λέγαμε	*πηγαίναμε*	*κρατούσαμε*
λέγατε	*πηγαίνατε*	*κρατούσατε*
ἔλεγαν or *λέγανε*	*πήγαιναν* or *πηγαίνανε*	*κρατοῦσαν* or *κρατούσανε*

Note that when a final *-ε* is added to the third person plural the augment is dropped.

The Imperfect denotes a continuous event in the past, e.g.

Ἡ νύχτα ἔπεφτε δροσερή, The night was coming down cool.

Ζητοῦσε τήν ἀδελφή του, He was looking for his sister.

Μιλοῦσαν γιά πολλή ὥρα, They were talking for a long time.

VOCABULARY

φτάνω, I reach
τό κέντρο, club
ὁ χορός, dance
κοιτάζω, look
καθώς, as
τραγουδῶ, I sing
τρέχω, I run
πέφτω, I fall
χάμω, on the ground
ἥσυχος, quiet
γκρίζος, grey
τό μυαλό, brain
ψυχρά, coldly
μαζί, together
προσπαθῶ, try
βρίσκω, I find
πνευματικός, mental
τό ἐπίπεδο, level
ἐνῶ, while
ἡ σκάλα, staircase
ἡ στιγμή, moment
καλά, well
σαχλός, inane, fatuous

EXERCISE 25

Translate:

1. *Ἀπό ἕνα κέντρο ἔφτανε μουσική χοροῦ.*
2. *Ἡ Λιλίκα δέν καταλάβαινε.*

3. *'Εκείνη τόν κοίταζε στά μάτια.*
4. *Καθώς πήγαινα στή δουλειά εἶδα τό Γιῶργο.*
5. *Τραγουδοῦσε ὅλο τό ἀπόγευμα.*
6. *Καθώς ἔτρεχα ἔπεσα χάμω.*
7. *Ὁ χοντρός ἔμενε ἥσυχος.*
8. *Μιλοῦσε μέ τό κορίτσι μέ τά γκρίζα μάτια.*
9. *Οἱ ἄλλοι δέ μιλοῦσαν.*
10. *Τό μυαλό του δούλευε ψυχρά.*
11. *Δέν ἔμεναν μαζί τους.*
12. *Προσπαθοῦσε νά βρεῖ τό πνευματικό ἐπίπεδο τοῦ παιδιοῦ.*
13. *'Ενώ ἀνέβαινε τή σκάλα ἄκουσε δυνατές φωνές.*
14. *Ὁ Χαράλαμπος ἔπινε μόνος του στό μπάρ.*
15. *Ὁ Ἄλκης ἄναβε ἐκείνη τή στιγμή τό τσιγάρο του.*
16. *Ἀπό μέρες ἡ μηχανή τοῦ αὐτοκινήτου του δέν πήγαινε καλά.*
17. *Ἔβρισκε σαχλό τό νεαρό.*

THE USE OF *νά*

Intention, hope, desire and the like are expressed by using the particle *νά* in front of (1) the Present, (2) the Indefinite and (3) the Imperfect as follows:

1. The particle *νά* in front of the Present tense expresses a continuous intention, etc., e.g. *Θέλω νά δουλεύω ἕξι ὧρες τήν ἡμέρα*, I want to be working six hours a day. *Ἄρχισε νά τραγουδᾶ*, He started singing.
2. The particle *νά* in front of the Indefinite expresses a non-continuous future intention, etc. This is the most frequent construction of this kind, e.g. *Ἐλπίζω νά φτάσω στήν Ἀθήνα στίς τρεῖς μ.μ.*, I hope to arrive at Athens at 3 p.m. *Μπορῶ νά πάρω ἕνα τσιγάρο;* May I take a cigarette?
3. The particle *νά* with the Imperfect expresses a past intention, etc. Such constructions follow a previous Imperfect tense, e.g. *Χτές τό βράδυ ἤθελα νά πήγαινα στό θέατρο ἀλλά δέν μπόρεσα*, Last night I wanted to go to the theatre but I did not manage to.

It is obvious that the above constructions follow verbs such as *θέλω*, *μπορῶ*, *ἐλπίζω*, etc. The same applies to certain verbs which are commonly used only in the third person singular and which correspond to English phrases consisting of " it is " and an adjective, e.g. *πρέπει*, it is necessary; *ἀξίζει*, it is worth while, etc.; e.g. *Πρέπει νά πηγαίνω τώρα*, I must be going now; *Πρέπει νά πάω στό γιατρό στίς τέσσερεις καί τριάντα*, I must go to the doctor at 4.30.

VOCABULARY

μπορῶ, I can
πρέπει, it is necessary
ἀγαπῶ, I love
τό ταξί, taxi
ἀξίζει, it is worth it
χωρίς, without
τό φλυντζάνι, cup
ἡ Ἀκρόπολις, Acropolis
χάνω, I lose
ἡ εὐτυχία, happiness
ἀμέσως, immediately
τό σχολεῖο, school
τά σταφύλια, grapes
τό τσάϊ, tea

EXERCISE 26

Translate:

1. *Μπορῶ νά πάω αὔριο;*
2. *Ἤθελε νά μιλήσει ἀλλά δέ μποροῦσε.*
3. *Τώρα πρέπει νά φύγετε.*
4. *Δέν ξέρω νά μιλῶ καλά ἀλλά αὐτό θέλω νά πῶ, «Ὅλοι ἀγαποῦμε τή δουλειά μας».*
5. *Μπορεῖτε νά πάρετε ἕνα ταξί.*
6. *Ὁ Ζήνων ἄρχισε νά τρέχει.*
7. *Δέν ἀξίζει νά πᾶτε στήν Ἀθήνα χωρίς νά δεῖτε τήν Ἀκρόπολη.*
8. *Δέ μποροῦσε νά κλείσει μάτι.*
9. *Τί θέλεις νά πεῖς;*
10. *Δέ θέλω νά πῶ τίποτε.*
11. *Δέν ἤθελε νά χάσει τήν εὐτυχία του.*
12. *Πρέπει νά φύγεις ἀμέσως.*

EXERCISE 27

1. I don't want to go to school.
2. May I have a cup of tea, please?
3. Can you give me a glass of water?
4. He didn't want to go to the pictures with you.

5. I must read this book tonight.
6. He started to laugh.
7. I want to eat grapes.
8. They did not want to lose their money.

THE PERFECT TENSES

The Present Perfect tense is formed by the auxiliary verb *ἔχω* conjugated as usual, and a form of the main verb which is identical with the third person singular of the Indefinite, e.g.

ἔχω	*χάσει,*	I have lost
ἔχεις	*χάσει,*	you have lost
ἔχει	*χάσει,*	he has lost
ἔχουμε	*χάσει,*	we have lost
ἔχετε	*χάσει,*	you have lost
ἔχουν	*χάσει,*	they have lost

The Past Perfect tense is formed in the same way as the Present Perfect but by replacing *ἔχω* by the Past form *εἶχα*, e.g.

εἶχα	*χάσει,*	I had lost
εἶχες	*χάσει,*	you had lost
εἶχε	*χάσει,*	he had lost
εἴχαμε	*χάσει,*	we had lost
εἴχατε	*χάσει,*	you had lost
εἶχαν	*χάσει,*	they had lost

The Present Perfect tense is not as common in Greek as it is in English, mainly because the work of the English Perfect is usually done by the Past tense in Greek, e.g.

Have you seen my brother, *Εἶδες τόν ἀδελφό μου;*

The Present Perfect tense is used to denote an event of the past which has a bearing on the present, e.g.

Δέ θέλω ἄλλο κρασί. Ἔχω πιεῖ πολύ, I do not want any more wine. I have drunk a lot.

The Past Perfect tense is more frequent than the Present Perfect. It aenotes an event of the past which occurred before another event of the past, e.g.

Πῆγα στό σπίτι του ἀλλά ἐκεῖνος εἶχε φύγει, I went to his house but he had left.

VOCABULARY

ἡ ἔκπληξη, surprise
σβύνω, I put out (the light)
ὁλότελα, completely
ὁ θυμός, anger
ἀποχτῶ, I acquire
τό ἔργο, work
ἡ τέχνη, art
περιμένω, I wait
τά νέα, news
ποτέ, never
ἐκεῖ, there

EXERCISE 28

Translate:

1. *Ἔχω χάσει ὅλα μου τά χρήματα.*
2. *Ἡ ἔκπληξη εἶχε σβύσει ὁλότελα τό θυμό του.*
3. *Ἔχασε τήν ὥρα του ἀλλά εἶχε ἀποχτήσει ἕνα καλό φίλο.*
4. *Δέν ἔχω δεῖ αὐτό τό ἔργο τέχνης.*
5. *Εἶχε ἀνάψει τό τσιγάρο του καί περίμενε.*
6. *Δέν εἶχαν ἀκούσει τά νέα.*
7. *Δέν εἶχες κλείσει τήν πόρτα.*
8. *Δέν ἔχω πάει ποτέ μου ἐκεῖ.*

THE IMPERATIVE

The Imperative form is another significant variation of the verb. It expresses command or request and occurs in the second person. In the singular it is formed by changing the final -*ω* of the Indefinite into -*ε* and removing the accent to the previous syllable whenever there is one, e.g. Indef. *ἀρχίσω*; Imper. *ἄρχισε*, start. Indef. *προσπαθήσω*; Imper. *προσπάθησε*, try. Indef. *δόσω*; Imper. *δόσε*, give. Indef. *βάλω*; Imper. *βάλε*, put. In the plural it is formed by changing -*ω* into -*τε* or sometimes -*ετε*, i.e. by using the form of the second person plural, *ἀρχίστε* or *ἀρχίσετε*, start; *προσπαθῆστε*, try; *δόστε*, give; *βάλτε*, put.

Some monosyllable forms add a final *ς* to the Imperative of the singular which may be retained in front of the ending of the plural, e.g. *πές*, say; *δές*, see; *πέστε*, say (pl.).

Some of class II verbs may replace the singular ending -*ησε* or -*ασε* by the ending *α*, e.g. *προχώρησε* or *προχώρα*, proceed; *χαμογέλασε* or *χαμογέλα*, smile; *μίλησε* or *μίλα*, speak.

The plural of such forms ends in -*ᾶτε* accented, e.g. *μιλᾶτε*, speak; *χαμογελᾶτε*, smile.

Another way of forming the Imperative, especially when the command implies a continuous event, is to use the form of the Present as the basis and treat it in the same way as the Indefinite, e.g. *γράφε*, write, or write and keep on writing; *βλέπε*, see, or see and keep seeing; *γράφετε*, write (pl.); *βλέπετε*, see (pl.). In the case of verbs of class II the final -*ω* of the Present is changed into -*α* and the accent is removed to the previous syllable. These forms are not different from the non-continuous forms, e.g. *προχώρα*, proceed; *σταμάτα*, stop.

Some common but irregular Imperatives are *ἔλα*, come, pl. *ἐλᾶτε*, come; *ἄσε*, pl. *ἄστε*, abandon (leave alone); *ἀνέβα*, go up, *κατέβα*, go down.

Another way of expressing command or request is by using *νά* and the second person of the Indefinite, e.g. *νά γράψεις*, (you must) write; *νά γράψετε*, (you must) write (pl.). In the case of a more continuous event *νά* is used with the Present, e.g. *νά γράφεις*, you must be writing; *νά γράφετε*, you must be writing, (pl.).

Negative command or request is expressed by *μή* and the second person of the Indefinite, e.g. *μή γράψεις*, do not write; *μή γράψετε* (pl.). For continuous events *μή* is used with the Present, e.g. *μή γράφεις*, do not go on writing; *μή γράφετε* (pl.). The particle *νά* may also precede the *μή*, e.g. *νά μή γράψεις*, do not write.

VOCABULARY

ἄσε, leave
τό ἀστεῖο, joke
φέρω, bring
γράφω, I write
σιγά, slowly
κατεβαίνω, I go down
κάτω, down
γρήγορα, quickly
τά αὐτιά, ears
ρίχνω, I throw
ἡ μπάλα, ball

EXAMPLES

Ἔλα ἐδῶ, Come here.
Πήγαινε ἐκεῖ, Go there.
Ἀκοῦστε τί θά σᾶς πῶ, Listen to what I am going to say to you.
Ξύπνα, Wake up.
Νά φύγεις, Go away.
Μή προχωρήσεις, Do not proceed.

EXERCISE 29

Translate:

1. *Κλεῖσε τά μάτια σου.*
2. *Κλεῖστε τά μάτια σας.*
3. *Ἄσε τά ἀστεῖα.*
4. *Γιά δές τί ἔφερα.*
5. *Πήγαινε στή δουλειά σου.*
6. *Ἔλα νά δεῖς μέ τά μάτια σου.*
7. *Ξύπνα καί εἶναι ἡ ὥρα δέκα.*
8. *Γράψε τό ὄνομά σου.*
9. *Σταμάτα ἐδῶ.*
10. *Ἀρχίστε νά τραγουδᾶτε.*
11. *Νά γράψεις αὐτά τά γράμματα.*
12. *Νά πᾶτε στό θεῖο σας.*
13. *Νά μείνεις ἐδῶ.*
14. *Μή σβύσεις τό φῶς.*
15. *Μή πεῖς τίποτε.*
16. *Νά μή φύγεις.*
17. *Νά μή πᾶτε τώρα.*
18. *Μιλᾶτε σιγά, παρακαλῶ.*
19. *Ἀνέβα τή σκάλα.*
10. *Κατέβα κάτω.*

EXERCISE 30

Translate:

1. Do not run.
2. Run quickly.
3. Go slowly.
4. Listen to your father.
5. Close your ears.
6. Open the door.
7. Do not laugh (pl.).

8. Do not eat (sing.).
9. Go to your house.
10. Write.
11. Do not write.
12. You must not drink a lot of wine.
13. Do not talk.
14. Do not move your hands.
15. Stay here for half an hour.
16. Throw the ball.
17. Continue the story.
18. Do not leave me alone.

THE PRONOUNS 'HIM', 'HER', 'IT' AND 'THEM'

Nouns which are used as objects of verbs may be replaced by certain pronouns. As such nouns are mostly in the accusative case the pronouns which replace them are also in the accusative. One such pronoun, that of the third person, has three forms corresponding to the three classes of the noun. These forms are identical with the accusative of the three definite articles. They are:

	Singular	*Plural*
(M)	*τόν*, him	*τούς*, them
(F)	*τήν*, her	*τίς*, them
(N)	*τό*, it	*τά*, them

The above pronouns literally stand for nouns when the context makes the meaning clear. They are put in front of the verb, except when it is in the imperative, e.g.

Εἶδες τόν κῆπο; Τόν εἶδα, Have you seen the garden? I have seen it.

Εἶδες τή Μαίρη; Τήν εἶδα, Have you seen Mary? I have seen her.

Εἶδες τό βιβλίο μου; Τό εἶδα, Have you seen my book? I have seen it.

Ἀγαπᾶς τούς ἀδελφούς σου; Τούς ἀγαπῶ, Do you love your brothers? I love them.

Ἔκλεισες τίς πόρτες; Τίς ἔκλεισα, Have you closed the doors? I have closed them.

Πῆρες τά γράμματά μου; Τά πῆρα, Did you receive my letters? I received them.

Πάρε αὐτό τό ποτήρι. Κράτα το καλά, Take this glass. Hold it carefully.
Σταμάτα τους, Stop them.
Σταμάτα την, Stop her.

The genitive singular form of the third person pronoun is again identical with that of the definite article. In the plural it is identical with the accusative of the M article.

Singular	*Plural*
(M) *τοῦ*	*τούς*
(F) *τῆς*	*τούς*
(N) *τοῦ*	*τούς*

The genitive is used when the verb may take two objects. In such cases the object which can be replaced by a prepositional construction is in the genitive case, and the other object is in the accusative. This happens whether the objects are nouns or pronouns, e.g.

Ἔδοσα τοῦ Γιώργου ἕνα βιβλίο, I gave George a book.

The genitive could be replaced as follows:

Ἔδοσα ἕνα βιβλίο στό Γιῶργο, I gave a book to George.

When the objects are pronouns the genitive is put in front of the accusative and also in front of the verb, e.g.

τοῦ τό ἔδωσα, I gave it to him (literally = to him it I gave).
τῆς εἶπε μιάν ἱστορία, he told her a story; *τῆς εἶπε*, he told her.
θά σοῦ δόσει δέκα δραχμές, he will give you ten drachmas.
τοῦ τό ἔγραψα, I wrote it to him (or for him).

When the verb is in the imperative the pronouns are put

after it and drop the accent or remove it to the previous syllable,* e.g.

Δόσε της λίγο νερό, Give her some water.
Πάρε μου ένα βιβλίο, Get a book for me.

* The accent is removed when the previous word has the accent on the third syllable from the end, e.g. *Άνοιξέ του τήν πόρτα*, Open the door for him.

THE PRONOUNS 'ME', 'YOU', 'US'

The first and second persons of the genitive case of the above pronoun are:

	Singular	*Plural*
1.	*μοῦ*	*μᾶς*
2.	*σοῦ*	*σᾶς*

The first and second persons of the accusative case are:

	Singular	*Plural*
1.	*μέ*	*μᾶς*
2.	*σέ*	*σᾶς*

EXAMPLES

Μοῦ εἶπε, He told me.
Σέ εἶδα, I saw you.
Θά σοῦ στείλω τά πράματα, I shall send you the things.
Σᾶς εὐχαριστῶ, I thank you.
Κοίταξέ με στά μάτια, Look me in the eyes.
Μή μοῦ τηλεφωνήσεις, Do not telephone to me.
Δόσε μου ἕνα τσιγάρο, Give me a cigarette.
Μᾶς ἔφερε πολλά πράματα, He brought (to) us many things.
Θά σᾶς πάρω στήν 'Ιταλία, I will take you to Italy.

The genitive of the pronoun (without a written accent) may also be used after certain prepositions, adverbs or adjectives, e.g. *μαζί μου*, with me; *κοντά του*, near him; *πάνω σου*, on you; *ποτέ μου*, never (in my life); *μόνος του*, alone (by himself); *δικός μου*, mine.*

The genitive is also used after words denoting greeting,

* See page 42.

e.g. *Καλημέρα σας*, Good morning to you; *Καληνύκτα σας*, Good night; *Γειά σου*, Good-bye (to one person); *Γειά σας*, Good-bye (to several persons).

VOCABULARY

ξοδεύω, I spend
πιάνω, I take hold of (grasp)
ἡ ποιότητα, quality
ἰδιωτικός, private
ἡ θέση, position
ἀγοράζω, I buy
τό βιβλίο, book
ὁ Ρῶσσος, Russian
σφίγγω, I squeeze
δίπλα, beside
ψάχνω, I look for
παρατῶ, I abandon
φωνάζω, I cry
ἡ ἀλήθεια, truth
πιστεύω, I believe
νομίζω, I think
γύρω, round
τηλεφωνῶ, I ring up
δίνω, I give
τό γραμματόσημο, stamp
τό κομμάτι, piece
τό χαρτί, paper
δείχνω, I show, point at
κάνω, I make, do
λένε,* they call, say

EXERCISE 31

Translate:

1. *Εἶχε πολλά χρήματα ἀλλά τά ξόδεψε.*
2. *Σέ ξέρω πολύ καλά.*
3. *Μέ λένε Λίλιαν.*
4. *Τόν ἔπιασε ἀπό τό χέρι καί τοῦ μίλησε.*
5. *Τόν ρωτοῦσε γιά τήν ποιότητα.*
6. *Ὁ πατέρας μου μέ ἔστειλε σέ ἰδιωτικό σχολεῖο.*

* The verb *λέγω* or *λέω* may also be declined as follows:

λέω, I say	*λέμε*, we say
λές, you say	*λέτε*, you say
λέει, he says	*λένε*, they say

In the same way the second person singular of *θέλω*, I want, may also be *θές*, you want.

7. *Δέν τό περίμενε.*
8. *Τόν κοίταξε στά μάτια.*
9. *Τόν ἔβαλε στή θέση του.*
10. *'Αγόρασα ἕνα βιβλίο καί τό διάβασα σέ μιά μέρα.*
11. *Δέν τό πίστευε.*
12. *Σέ παρακολουθῶ γιά πολύν καιρό.*
13. *Σέ νόμιζα Ρῶσσο.*
14. *Τοῦ ἔσφιξε τό χέρι.*
15. *Ἔμενε δίπλα του.*
16. *Δέν τό ἔχω δεῖ ποτέ μου.*
17. *Δέν τήν εἶχε καταλάβει.*
18. *Ἔψαχνε νά τόν βρεῖ.*
19. *Παράτα με.*
20. *Αὔριο, ξύπνα με νωρίς.*
21. *Ἄσε με νά φύγω.*
22. *Τόν εἶδε καί τοῦ φώναξε.*
23. *Πές μου τήν ἀλήθεια.*
24. *Μή μοῦ τά λές αὐτά.*
25. *Τήν βλέπεις;*
26. *Γιατί μοῦ τά λές αὐτά;*
27. *Θέλεις νά σοῦ δείξω τόν κῆπο;*
28. *Μένουν μαζί μας.*
29. *Σᾶς γνωρίζω ἀπό καιρό.*
30. *Δέ θά τό κάνεις.*
31. *Πήγαινε καί σέ περιμένουν.*
32. *Ἔτρεχαν γύρω του.*
33. *Ἔχω νά σοῦ πῶ κάμποσα ἄλλα.*
34. *Δέ μπορῶ νά τό κάνω.*
35. *Γιατί τόν ἀφίσατε νά φύγει;*
36. *Τηλεφώνησέ μου αὔριο τό πρωΐ.*
37. *Δός μου τρία γραμματόσημα.*
38. *Θά στό πῶ. (= Θά σοῦ τό πῶ.)*

EXERCISE 32

Translate:.

1. She turned and looked at him.
2. He did not tell me anything.
3. Go by yourself (alone).
4. Come beside me.
5. Fetch me a piece of paper.
6. They call me.
7. What did father say to you?
8. They asked him many questions.
9. Do ring me tonight.
10. Show me the garden.
11. You must always tell the truth.
12. I don't believe you.
13. Give me two bottles of beer.
14. I do not know him.
15. They didn't see him.
16. All the family is waiting for you.
17. Get a taxi for me.
18. Talk to me about this affair.
19. He went near them.
20. Good morning to you.

SUMMARY OF PRINCIPAL FORMS OF ACTIVE VERBS

I

	Present	*Indefinite*	*Past*	*Imperfect*
Sing.				
1.	ἀρχίζω	ἀρχίσω	ἄρχισα	ἄρχιζα
2.	ἀρχίζεις	ἀρχίσεις	ἄρχισες	ἄρχιζες
3.	ἀρχίζει	ἀρχίσει	ἄρχισε	ἄρχιζε
Plural				
1.	ἀρχίζουμε	ἀρχίσουμε	ἀρχίσαμε	ἀρχίζαμε
2.	ἀρχίζετε	ἀρχίσετε	ἀρχίσατε	ἀρχίζατε
3.	ἀρχίζουν	ἀρχίσουν	ἄρχισαν	ἄρχιζαν

II

Sing.				
1.	σταματῶ	σταματήσω	σταμάτησα	σταματοῦσα
2.	σταματᾶς	σταματήσεις	σταμάτησες	σταματοῦσες
3.	σταματᾶ	σταματήσει	σταμάτησε	σταματοῦσε
Plural				
1.	σταματοῦμε	σταματήσουμε	σταματήσαμε	σταματούσαμε
2.	σταματᾶτε	σταματήσετε	σταματήσατε	σταματούσατε
3.	σταματοῦν	σταματήσουν	σταμάτησαν	σταματοῦσαν

PASSIVE VERBS

Passive verbs are of two classes corresponding to the two classes of Active verbs:

I. Those ending in *-ομαι.*
II. Those ending in *-οῦμαι*, *-ᾶμαι* or *-ιέμαι.*

I. The Present tense of verbs of this class is conjugated as follows:

ἐξετάζομαι, I am examined
ἐξετάζεσαι, you are examined
ἐξετάζεται, he is examined
ἐξεταζόμαστε, we are examined
ἐξετάζεστε, you are examined
ἐξετάζονται, they are examined

Passive verbs can be grouped in approximately the same sub-classes as Active verbs. These sub-classes determine the form of the Indefinite in the following way:

I*a*. Verbs of this class form the Indefinite by changing

-ομαι into *-σθῶ**
-ζομαι into *-σθῶ*
-νομαι into *-θῶ*

e.g. *κλείνομαι*, I am closed; Indef. *κλεισθῶ.*
γνωρίζομαι, I am known; Indef. *γνωρισθῶ.*
ἐξετάζομαι, I am examined; Indef. *ἐξετασθῶ.*
χάνομαι, I am lost; Indef. *χαθῶ.*

* Final *-θῶ*, etc., may be replaced by *-τῶ*, etc.

I*b*. Verbs of this class form the Indefinite by changing

-*βομαι*	into -*φθῶ*
-*νομαι*	into -*νθῶ*
(pronounced *vome*)	(pronounced *ftho*)

e.g. *κρύβομαι*, I am hiding;	Indef. *κρυφθῶ*.
μαζεύομαι, I am picked up;	Indef. *μαζευθῶ*.

I*c*. Verbs of this class form the Indefinite by changing -*ζομαι*, -*γομαι*, -*χνομαι*, -*χομαι*, into -*χθῶ*.

e.g. *ἀλλάζομαι*, I am changed;	Indef. *ἀλλαχθῶ*.
ἀνοίγομαι, I am opened;	Indef. *ἀνοιχθῶ*.
δείχνομαι, I am shown;	Indef. *δειχθῶ*.
βρέχομαι, I get wet;	Indef. *βρεχθῶ*.

I*d*. Verbs of this class change -*ομαι* into -*θῶ*.

e.g. *φέρομαι*, I am brought;	Indef. *φερθῶ*.

I*e*. Verbs of this class being irregular form the Indefinite in the following individual ways:

βρίσκομαι, I am found;	Indef. *βρεθῶ*.
δίνομαι, I am given;	Indef. *δοθῶ*.
παίρνομαι, I am taken;	Indef. *παρθῶ*.
στέκομαι, I stand;	Indef. *σταθῶ*.
βάζομαι, I am put;	Indef. *βαλθῶ*.
τρώγομαι, I am eaten;	Indef. *φαγωθῶ*.
ἀντιλαμβάνομαι, I understand;	Indef. *ἀντιληφθῶ*.
φαίνομαι, I seem;	Indef. *φανῶ*.
χαίρομαι, I am glad;	Indef. *χαρῶ*.

The Indefinite is conjugated like Active verbs of class II*c*, e.g.

βρεθῶ	*βρεθοῦμε*
βρεθεῖς	*βρεθεῖτε*
βρεθεῖ	*βρεθοῦν*

The Past tense is formed by changing the final -*ῶ* of the Indefinite into -*ηκα* and removing the accent to the third syllable from the end, e.g.

Indefinite	*Past*	
ἐξεταστῶ	ἐξετάστηκα	I was examined
κλειστῶ	κλείστηκα	I was closed
χαθῶ	χάθηκα	I was lost
κρυφτῶ	κρύφτηκα	I hid myself
προσεχτῶ	προσέχτηκα	I was noticed
βρεθῶ	βρέθηκα	I was found
φανῶ	φάνηκα	I appeared
χαρῶ	χάρηκα	I was glad

The Past tense is conjugated like the Past tense of Active verbs, e.g.

Singular

βρέθηκα, I was found
βρέθηκες, you were found
βρέθηκε, he was found

Plural

βρεθήκαμε, we were found
βρεθήκατε, you were found
βρέθηκαν, they were found

The Imperfect tense is formed by changing the -*ομαι* of the Present into -*όμουνα*, e.g.

Present	*Imperfect*	
αἰσθάνομαι	αἰσθανόμουνα	I was feeling
χάνομαι	χανόμουνα	I was being lost
ἐξετάζομαι	ἐξεταζόμουνα	I was examined
βρίσκομαι	βρισκόμουνα	I was found

It is conjugated thus:

Singular

αἰσθανόμουνα, I was feeling
αἰσθανόσουνα, you were feeling
αἰσθανότανε, he was feeling

Plural

αἰσθανόμασταν, we were feeling
αἰσθανόσασταν, you were feeling
αἰσθανόντανε,
or *αἰσθανόντουσαν*, they were feeling

The Perfect and Past Perfect tenses are formed by putting *ἔχω* and *εἶχα* respectively in front of a form that is identical with the third person singular of the Indefinite, e.g.

	Perfect	*Past Perfect*
Sing.		
	ἔχω χαθεῖ, I have been lost	*εἶχα χαθεῖ*, I had been lost
	ἔχεις χαθεῖ, you have been lost	*εἶχες χαθεῖ*, you had been lost
	ἔχει χαθεῖ, he has been lost	*εἶχε χαθεῖ*, he had been lost
Plural		
	ἔχουμε χαθεῖ, we have been lost	*εἴχαμε χαθεῖ*, we had been lost
	ἔχετε χαθεῖ, you have been lost	*εἴχατε χαθεῖ*, you had been lost
	ἔχουν χαθεῖ, they have been lost	*εἶχαν χαθεῖ*, they had been lost

II. Passive verbs of class II end in *-οῦμαι*, *-ᾶμαι* or *-ιέμαι*. They are conjugated as follows:

Sing.

συγκινοῦμαι, I am moved	*κρατιέμαι*, I am held
συγκινεῖσαι, you are moved	*κρατιέσαι*, you are held
συγκινεῖται, he is moved	*κρατιέται*, he is held

φοβᾶμαι, I am afraid
φοβᾶσαι, you are afraid
φοβᾶται, he is afraid

Plural

συγκινούμαστε, we are moved	*κρατιόμαστε*, we are held
συγκινεῖστε, you are moved	*κρατιέστε*, you are held
συγκινοῦνται, they are moved	*κρατιοῦνται*, they are held

φοβόμαστε, we are afraid
φοβᾶστε, you are afraid
φοβοῦνται, they are afraid

The Indefinite is formed by changing the endings *-οῦμαι*, *-ᾶμαι* or *-ιέμαι* into *-ηθῶ*,

e.g. *συγκινηθῶ*
κρατηθῶ
φοβηθῶ

It is conjugated in the same way as the Indefinite of verbs of class I. All other tenses are formed and conjugated like those of verbs of class I, e.g.

συγκινήθηκα, I was moved
φοβήθηκα, I became afraid
εἶχα φοβηθεῖ, I had been scared

The Imperative of both class I and II verbs is formed by changing the -*ῶ* of the Indefinite into -*ου* and removing the accent to the previous syllable. -*θῶ* may be changed into -*σου*, while -*φθῶ* and -*ντῶ* may be changed into -*ψου*, e.g.

στάσου, stand up
κρατήσου, hold on
φάνου, appear
παντρέψου, get married
σκέψου, think

The Plural Imperative is formed by changing the -*ῶ* of the Indefinite into -*εῖτε*, e.g.

φανεῖτε, appear
σταθεῖτε, stand
σκεφθεῖτε, think

Negative command is expressed by *μή* and the Indefinite or the Present according to whether the action is fixed or continuous, e.g.

μή φοβηθεῖς, do not get afraid
μή φοβᾶσαι, do not be afraid
μή φοβηθεῖτε, don't get frightened

Passive verbs are comparatively rare in Greek. This is because events with a Passive meaning are usually expressed by Active verbs and the accusative of the personal pronoun, e.g.

I was stopped by my father, *Μέ σταμάτησε ὁ πατέρας μου* (lit. = My father stopped me).

When the subject is undefined the verb is in the plural, e.g. He was brought in, *Τόν φέρανε μέσα.*

VOCABULARY

ντρέπομαι, I am ashamed
θυμᾶμαι, I remember
φαίνομαι, I seem, appear
περήφανος, proud
βρίσκομαι, I am (found)
τό πάτωμα, floor
λυπᾶμαι, I am sorry
σηκώνομαι, I get up
ἀπότομα, suddenly
παραξενεύομαι, I am surprised
παντρεύομαι, I get married
φοβᾶμαι, I fear
στέκομαι, I stand
ἀπέναντι, opposite
περίφημος, famous
δίνομαι, I am given
συγκινημένος, moved, upset
φωτισμένος, lit
τό ζευγάρι, couple
χορεύω, I dance
ἑτοιμάζομαι, I get ready
ἀντιλαμβάνομαι, I understand, perceive
κοιμᾶμαι, I (go to) sleep
σκέφτομαι, I think (about)
χάνομαι, I get lost

EXERCISE 33

Translate:

1. *Ντρέπομαι γι' αὐτήν.*
2. *Μέ θυμᾶσαι;*
3. *Φαίνεσαι περήφανος γι'αὐτό.*
4. *Τώρα βρισκόμαστε στό ἕκτο πάτωμα.*
5. *Βρίσκεται στό γραφεῖο.*
6. *Σέ λυπᾶμαι.*
7. *Σηκώθηκε ἀπότομα.*
8. *Τό κορίτσι παραξενεύτηκε.*
9. *Ὁ Ἀλέκος παντρεύτηκε τή Βέρα.*
10. *Γιά πρώτη φορά ὁ Φίλιππος φοβήθηκε.*
11. *Στάθηκε ἀπέναντί του.*
12. *Τό περίφημο πάρτυ δόθηκε.*
13. *Βρέθηκε μόνος.*
14. *Ἐκείνη φαινόταν συγκινημένη.*

15. *Στεκόταν δίπλα του.*
16. *Σέ μιά φωτισμένη βεράντα φαίνονταν δυό ζευγάρια πού χόρευαν.*
17. *Ἑτοιμαζόταν νά φύγει.*
18. *Δέν τήν εἶχε ἀντιληφθεῖ.*
19. *Θέλει νά τήν παντρευτεῖ.*
20. *Δέν μποροῦσα νά κοιμηθῶ ὅλη νύχτα.*
21. *Κοιμήσου.*
22. *Σκέψου καλά.*
23. *Μήν ἑτοιμάζεσαι.*
24. *Στάσου ἐδῶ.*

EXERCISE 34

Translate:

1. I do not remember you.
2. I cannot think now.
3. I got very frightened.
4. I am not sorry for you.
5. She got ready very quickly.
6. He stood near me.
7. I cannot sleep these days.
8. Do not get lost.
9. Where is he (found) now?
10. Sleep.

MIXED VERBS

Some verbs such as ἔρχομαι, I come; κάθομαι, I sit; γίνομαι, I become, have a Passive form in the Present and an Active one in the Indefinite. Their main tenses are as follows:

Present		
ἔρχομαι, I come	κάθομαι, I sit	γίνομαι, I become
Indef.		
ἔρθω	καθίσω or κάτσω	γίνω
Past		
ἦρθα, I came	κάθισα, I sat	ἔγινα, I became
Imperfect		
ἐρχόμουνα, I was coming	καθόμουνα, I was sitting	γινόμουνα, I was becoming

Their Indefinite Imperative is

.ἔλα, come	κάθισε or κάτσε, sit	γίνου, become
ἐλᾶτε	καθῖστε	γενῆτε

A rather unique Passive verb is εἶμαι, I am, which is conjugated as follows:

	Present and Indefinite	*Past and Imperfect*
Sing.	εἶμαι, I am	ἤμουν or ἤμουνα, I was
	εἶσαι, you are	ἤσουν(α), you were
	εἶναι, he is	ἦταν(ε) he was
	εἴμαστε, we are	ἤμασταν, we were
	εἶστε, you are	ἤσασταν, you were
	εἶναι, they are	ἦταν(ε) they were

EXAMPLES

Ἦρθε στήν Ἑλλάδα μέ κάμποσα λεφτά, He came to Greece with a lot of money
Ἔρχεσαι μαζί μας; Are you coming with us?
Καθῖστε παρακαλῶ, Sit down please.
Ἤμουν πέντε χρονῶν, I was five years old.

VOCABULARY

εἶμαι, I am
χωρίς, without
ἡ θέληση, will
κουρασμένος, tired
χαμηλός, low
γίνομαι, I become
τί; what?
ἡ ὁμιλία, talk
ὁ μηχανικός, engineer
κάθομαι, I sit (down)
τό τραπεζάκι, small table

EXERCISE 35

Translate:

1. *Εἶσαι ἕνας ἄνθρωπος χωρίς θέληση.*
2. *Εἴμαστε πολύ κουρασμένοι.*
3. *Κάθισαν γύρω ἀπό ἕνα χαμηλό τραπεζάκι.*
4. *Θά ἔρθω αὔριο.*
5. *Καθόταν δίπλα του.*
6. *Τοῦ εἶπε νά καθίσει.*
7. *Ἤμουν τότε ἐννέα χρονῶν.*
8. *Δέν ἤξερε τί γινόταν.*
9. *Μή καθίσεις ἐκεῖ.*
10. *Ἐλᾶτε νά πᾶμε στό θέατρο.*
11. *Ἡ ὁμιλία σας ἦταν περίφημη.*
12. *Θά γίνω μηχανικός.*
13. *Εἶναι δικό μου.*
14. *Τί θέλετε παρακαλῶ;*

THE PRONOUNS 'I', 'YOU', 'HE', ETC.

As has been stated, person is denoted by the ending of verbs. Sometimes, however, especially when emphasis or explicitness is required, the personal pronoun is used. Its forms are:

ἐγώ, I	*ἐμεῖς*, we
ἐσύ, you	*ἐσεῖς*, you
αὐτός, he	*αὐτοί*, they

e.g. *'Εγώ πῆγα στήν 'Αγγλία*, I went to England.
Σεῖς δέν ἤρθατε, You did not come.

Another form of the accusative case of the personal pronoun* is *ἐμένα*, me; *ἐμᾶς*, us; *ἐσένα* or *σένα*, you; *ἐσᾶς* or *σᾶς*, you; e.g.

κοντά σ' ἐμένα, near me.
Μιλοῦσε σ' ἐσᾶς, He was talking to you.

The above pronouns usually answer the interrogative adjective *ποιός*, who? (gen. *ποιανοῦ*, whose), e.g.

Ποιός ἔφαγε τά πορτοκάλια; Who has eaten the oranges?
'Εγώ, I (did).
Ποιοί εἶναι 'Ιταλοί; Who are Italians?
'Εμεῖς οἱ τρεῖς, We three.

OTHER USES OF *ποιός*, ETC.

Ποιανοῦ εἶναι τό αὐτοκίνητο; Whose is the car?
Εἶναι δικό μου, It is mine.

* See page 100.

Σέ ποιούς ἔδοσα χρήματα; To whom have I given money? *Σέ μᾶς,* To us.

Note that *τί*, what? (gen. *τίνος*), is another common interrogative adjective, e.g.

Τί εἶναι αὐτό; What is this?
Τίνος εἶναι αὐτά τά παπούτσια; Whose are these shoes?

The Greek equivalent of English reflexive pronouns such as " myself ", " yourself ", etc. is the noun *ὁ ἑαυτός* followed by the appropriate possessive pronoun, *μου*, my, *σου*, your, etc. This phrase usually occurs as the object of verbs, e.g.

Βλέπω τόν ἑαυτό μου, I see myself.
Αὐτή ἡ γυναίκα βλέπει τόν ἑαυτό της στόν καθρέφτη, This woman sees herself in the mirror.

VOCABULARY

ποιός, who?
τίνος, whose?
μισῶ, I hate
ὁ ἑαυτός, oneself
ὁ ἑκατομμυριοῦχος, millionaire
τό ρολόϊ, clock, watch
ἐγώ, I
ἐμεῖς, we
ἐσεῖς, you (pl.)

EXERCISE 36

Translate:

1. *Ποιόν θέλετε;*
2. *'Εσεῖς, τί νομίζετε;*
3. *Τίνος εἶναι αὐτό τό καπέλλο;*
4. *Μισῶ τόν ἑαυτό μου.*
5. *Θά δόσω τρεῖς δραχμές σέ σένα καί τρεῖς στόν ἀδελφό σου.*

6. *Ἐμεῖς δέν εἴμαστε ἑκατομμυριοῦχοι.*
7. *Σέ ποιόν ἔδωσα τό ρολόϊ μου;*
8. *Ἐμᾶς μή μᾶς ρωτᾶς.*
9. *Ἐγώ τό εἶπα.*
10. *Ἐγώ ξέρω τόν ἑαυτό μου.*
11. *Ποιανοῦ εἶναι αὐτό τό κουτί τά σπίρτα;*

SUMMARY OF THE DIFFERENT FORMS OF PRONOUNS*

Nominative	*Genitive*
1. ἐγώ, I	1. μοῦ, my
2. ἐσύ, you (familiar)	2. σοῦ, your
3. αὐτός, he	3. τοῦ, his
αὐτή, she	τῆς, her
αὐτό, it	τοῦ, its
1. ἐμεῖς, we	1. μᾶς, our
2. ἐσεῖς, you	2. σᾶς, your
3. αὐτοί, they	3. τούς, their
αὐτές, they	
αὐτά, they	

Accusative

	or	
1. μέ, me		μένα
2. σέ, you		σένα
3. τόν, him		αὐτόν
τήν, her		αὐτήν
τό, it		αὐτό
1. μᾶς, us		(ἐ)μᾶς
2. σᾶς, you		(ἐ)σᾶς
3. τούς, them		αὐτούς
τίς, them		αὐτές
τά, them		αὐτά

* These pronouns have been dealt with separately in previous chapters (see pp. 39, 42, 97, 100, 115).

PART TWO
INVARIABLE WORDS

ADVERBS

There are only about two hundred invariable words, but, being in very frequent use, they are most important. They are mostly very short words. The best way to classify them is by considering their place and function in the sentence. Thus words that are usually put after verbs in order to modify them are called adverbs, e.g.

Τά παιδιά ἔτρεξαν ἐκεῖ, The children ran there.
Μιλᾶτε σιγά, Speak slowly.

Most words that can replace *ἐκεῖ* or *σιγά* in the above or equivalent sentences are adverbs, e.g.

Τά παιδιά ἔτρεξαν πολύ, The children ran a lot.
Τά παιδιά ἔτρεξαν γρήγορα, The children ran fast.
Μή μιλᾶτε τώρα, Do not speak now.

The commonest adverbs are the following:

ἐδῶ, here
ἐκεῖ, there
πάνω, up
κάτω, down
πίσω, behind
μπροστά, in front
ἀλλοῦ, somewhere else
τώρα, now
ὕστερα, after, later
νωρίς, early
αὔριο, tomorrow
μαζί, together
λίγο, a little
πολύ, a lot
ἄλλοτε, previously
κάποτε, sometimes, then
κιόλας, already
ποτέ, never
πάλιν, again
πρίν, earlier
τότε, then
ἴσως, perhaps
χθές, yesterday
πάντοτε, always
ἀλλιῶς, otherwise
ἀκόμα, yet
ἔτσι, thus
σιγά, slowly

Many adverbs are formed from adjectives by changing the final *-ος* into *-α*, e.g.

Adjective	*Adverb*
ἥσυχος, quiet	*ἥσυχα*, quietly
καλός, good	*καλά*, well
εὔκολος, easy	*εὔκολα*, easily
ἀρκετός, sufficient	*ἀρκετά*, sufficiently, rather
γρήγορος, quick	*γρήγορα*, quickly
ἀριστερός, left	*ἀριστερά*, to the left

Adjectives that are in the comparative or superlative forms can produce adverbs in the same way, e.g.

καλύτερος, better	*καλύτερα*, better
χειρότερος, worse	*χειρότερα*, worse
εὐκολότατος, most easy	*εὐκολότατα*, most easily

VOCABULARY

περπατῶ, I walk
συχνά, often
ἡ τηλεόραση, television
τό ταξίδι, journey, trip
δεξιά, to the right
καθαρός, clean, clear
τά γυαλιά, spectacles
ἐξετάζω, I examine
διαπεραστικά, piercingly
λησμονῶ, I forget
ἴσια, straight on
ἀργά, late, slowly
κλαίω, Indef. *κλάψω*, I cry
περίεργος, strange, curious

EXAMPLES

Περπάτα σιγά, Walk slowly.
Παρακολουθεῖτε συχνά τηλεόραση; Do you watch television often?
Τό μυαλό του δούλευε ψυχρά, His brain worked coolly.
Αὔριο θά πᾶμε ταξίδι, Tomorrow we shall go on a journey.

Πηγαίνετε δεξιά, Go right.
Εὐχαριστῶ πολύ, Thanks a lot.

EXERCISE 37

Translate:

1. *Εἶχε πάντοτε λεφτά.*
2. *Πηγαίνετε ἀπέναντι καί ρωτᾶτε.*
3. *Ἄφισε ἥσυχα τό ποτήρι του στό τζάκι.*
4. *Βλέπω καθαρά μ' αὐτά τά γυαλιά.*
5. *Τόν ἐξέταζε διαπεραστικά.*
6. *Εἶναι κιόλας δεκαπέντε χρονῶν.*
7. *Τί θές νά κάνουμε, εἶπε ἀπότομα.*
8. *Τήν εἶχε ὁλότελα λησμονήσει.*
9. *Κάνετε γρήγορα.*
10. *Πήγαμε μαζί ἀλλ' ἐκεῖνος γύρισε πίσω.*
11. *Νά πᾶτε ἴσια κι' ὕστερα δεξιά.*
12. *Ὁ Γιῶργος κοιμᾶται ἀργά καί ξυπνᾶ νωρίς τό πρωΐ.*
13. *Μοῦ κουνοῦσε τό χέρι του, ἔτσι.*

EXERCISE 38

Translate:

1. Come here quickly.
2. Come back now.
3. He has eaten and drunk enough.
4. You had better come tomorrow.
5. He hasn't come.
6. Walk very slowly.
7. Come again.
8. Now you laugh but later you will cry.
9. Tomorrow he will be better.
10. He was looking at her curiously.

Some adverbs that are formed from adjectives end in -ως. This happens mostly when the adjectives end in -ης.*

The following are some of the commonest adverbs formed in this way:

Adjective	*Adverb*
ἀκριβής, exact	ἀκριβῶς, exactly
εἰλικρινής, sincere	εἰλικρινῶς, sincerely
συνήθης, usual	συνήθως, usually
εὐτυχής, happy	εὐτυχῶς, luckily

Some adjectives ending in -ος form adverbs in both -α and -ως.

τέλειος, perfect	τελείως, completely, or τέλεια, perfectly
ἁπλός, simple	ἁπλῶς or ἁπλά, simply
ἔκτακτος, occasional	ἐκτάκτως or ἔκτακτα, occasionally

Some adjectives end in -υς.† They form adverbs ending in -ιά, e.g.

βαθύς, deep	βαθιά, deeply
μακρύς, long	μακριά, far
πλατύς, wide	πλατιά, widely

* There are very few such adjectives, such as ἀκριβής, exact; εἰλικρινής, sincere. They are declined as follows:

Sing. (*M.* & *F.*)	*Sing.* (*N.*)
εἰλικρινής	εἰλικρινές
εἰλικρινῆ or εἰλικρινοῦς	εἰλικρινοῦς
εἰλικρινῆ	εἰλικρινές
Plural	*Plural*
εἰλικρινεῖς	εἰλικρινῆ
εἰλικρινῶν	εἰλικρινῶν
εἰλικρινεῖς	εἰλικρινῆ

† Footnote on opposite page.

VOCABULARY

δῶ = ἐδῶ, here
ἡ Νέα 'Υόρκη, New York
συνεπής, consistent
συνεπῶς, consequently
ὁ συγγραφέας, writer
τό ποτάμι, river
διαρκῶς, continuously
τί; what?

EXAMPLES

Εἶναι ἡ ὥρα δώδεκα ἀκριβῶς, It is twelve o'clock exactly.
Εὐτυχῶς τό δωμάτιο εἶναι ζεστό, Luckily the room is warm.
Ἔκλεισε τελείως τά μάτια του, He closed his eyes completely.

EXERCISE 39

Translate:

1. *Πήγαινε ἐκεῖ συνήθως τά ἀπογεύματα.*
2. *'Η Νέα 'Υόρκη εἶναι πολύ μακριά ἀπό δῶ.*

† They are declined as follows:

	M	F	N
Sing.	ὁ βαθύς	ἡ βαθειά	τό βαθύ
	τοῦ βαθιοῦ	τῆς βαθειᾶς	τοῦ βαθιοῦ
	τό βαθύ	τή βαθειά	τό βαθύ
Plural	οἱ βαθιοί	οἱ βαθειές	τά βαθιά
	τῶν βαθιῶν	τῶν βαθειῶν	τῶν βαθιῶν
	τούς βαθιούς	τίς βαθειές	τά βαθιά

A quite individual adjectival ending in -υς is *πολύς*, much, which has already been used in some of its forms and which is declined as follows:

	M	F	N
Sing.	ὁ πολύς	ἡ πολλή	τό πολύ
	τοῦ πολλοῦ	τῆς πολλῆς	τοῦ πολλοῦ
	τόν πολύ	τήν πολλή	τό πολύ
Plural	οἱ πολλοί	οἱ πολλές	τά πολλά
	τῶν πολλῶν	τῶν πολλῶν	τῶν πολλῶν
	τούς πολλούς	τίς πολλές	τά πολλά

3. *Σᾶς μιλῶ εἰλικρινῶς.*
4. *Δυστυχῶς δέν ἔχω λεφτά μαζί μου.*
5. *Θά ἔρθω στίς τρεῖς ἀκριβῶς.*
6. *Δέ μᾶς γράψατε· συνεπῶς δέν ἤρθαμε.*
7. *Ὁ Χάρης εἶναι πολύ συνεπής καί εἰλικρινής ἀλλά δέν εἶναι ἀκριβής στήν ὥρα του.*
8. *Ὁ Σαίξπηρ εἶναι ἕνας βαθύς συγγραφέας.*
9. *Αὐτό τό ποτάμι εἶναι πολύ βαθύ.*
0. *Νά φύγετε. Ἀλλιῶς θά σᾶς διώξουμε.*
11. *Μιλοῦσε διαρκῶς ἀλλά δέν καταλάβαινα τί ἔλεγε.*
12. *Θέλω ἁπλῶς νά μέ ἀφίσετε ἥσυχο.*
13. *Συνήθως δέν πάω στό σινεμά, ἀλλά χθές πῆγα ἐκτάκτως.*

ACTIVE PARTICIPLES

Some adverbs are formed from verbs by changing the final *-ω* of Active verbs into *-οντας* for verbs of class I, and *-ώντας* for verbs of class II, e.g.

κλαίω, I cry	*κλαίοντας*, crying
γελῶ, I laugh	*γελώντας*, laughing

EXAMPLES

Τά παιδιά έτρεχαν κλαίοντας, The children were running, crying.

Τά παιδιά έτρεχαν γελώντας, The children were running, laughing.

These adverbs are said to be the Participles of Active verbs and they may partly behave like verbs in that they can take their own objects, e.g.

Ἔφυγε κουνώντας τά χέρια του, He went away waving his hands.

Active Participles are rarer in Greek than in English because the Greek Present and Imperfect tenses express both instantaneous and continuous events, e.g.

Τώρα τρώγω, Now I am eating.
Τραγουδοῦσε, He was singing.

Active Participles are used to modify verbs which are mostly in the Imperfect and Past tenses.

VOCABULARY

τινάζω, I push away
ἡ καρέκλα, chair
τό θέμα, subject
ἀπαντῶ, I answer
τό βλέμμα, look
ἀθόρυβα, noiselessly
τονίζω, I stress
ξαπλώνω, I lie down
λίγο, a while
ἀνατολικά, eastwards
εὔθυμος, gay
ἀλλάζω, change
ἡ σημασία, meaning, sense
ἀποφεύγω, I avoid
πλησιάζω, I approach
ἡ πρόταση, sentence
φτάνω, I arrive, reach
τό ταβάνι, ceiling
ὁ διευθυντής, director
χωρίς, without

EXERCISE 40

Translate:

1. *Σηκώθηκε ἀπότομα τινάζοντας τήν καρέκλα πίσω του.*
2. *Σᾶς εὐχαριστῶ, εἶπε χαμογελώντας.*
3. *Πήγαινε τραγουδώντας.*
4. *Ἄλλοι πίνοντας γίνονται εὔθυμοι.*
5. *Μιλοῦσε ἀλλάζοντας θέματα χωρίς σημασία.*
6. *Ὄχι, ἀπάντησε αὐτός, ἀποφεύγοντας τό βλέμμα της.*
7. *Εἶχε πλησιάσει ἀθόρυβα καί τούς παρακολουθοῦσε χαμογελώντας.*
8. *Ἐπανάλαβε τήν πρόταση τονίζοντας κάθε λέξη.*
9. *Περπατοῦσε κοιτάζοντας πίσω του.*
10. *Μιλοῦσε διαρκῶς κουνώντας τό χέρι της.*

EXERCISE 41

Translate:

1. I shall go running.
2. He came singing in a loud voice.

3. He arrived without being able to say a word.
4. He lay down looking at the ceiling.
5. They sat for a while, talking to the director.
6. They left, going eastwards.

PASSIVE PARTICIPLES*

The Participle of Passive verbs is formed by changing the final -*θῶ* or -*τῶ* of the Indefinite into -*μένος*, e.g.

Present	*Indefinite*	*Participle*	
χάνομαι	*χαθῶ*	*χαμένος*	lost
ἁπλώνομαι	*ἁπλωθῶ*	*ἁπλωμένος*	spread
κουράζομαι	*κουραστῶ*	*κουρασμένος*	tired

If there is *χ* or *φ* in front of -*θω* or -*τω* they are changed into *γ* and *μ* respectively, e.g.

Present	*Indefinite*	*Participle*	
ἀλλάζυμαι	*ἀλλαχθῶ*	*ἀλλαγμένος*	changed
κρύβομαι	*κρυφθῶ*	*κρυμμένος*	hidden

Passive Participles are adjectives both in the way they are declined and in the way they behave in sentences. Thus, there are three classes of Participles declined like adjectives ending in -*ος*.

M	*F*	*N*
ὁ κουρασμένος, tired	*ἡ κουρασμένη*	*τό κουρασμένο*
ὁ κρατημένος, reserved	*ἡ κρατημένη*	*τό κρατημένο*

Some frequent but irregular Passive Participles are *χαρούμενος*, happy, from *χαίρομαι*, I am happy, glad; *κοιμισμένος*, asleep, from *κοιμᾶμαι*, I am sleeping; *πεθαμένος*, dead, from *πεθαίνω*, I die.

Some Passive Participles are based on verbs which are more common in the Active form, e.g. *τρομαγμένος*, scared, from *τρομάζω*, I get scared; *μεθυσμένος*, drunk,

* In contrast to the general heading of this section, passive participles are variable parts of speech.

from μεθῶ, I get drunk; θυμωμένος, angry, from θυμώνω, I get angry.

Some adjectives end in -μένος on the analogy of Passive Participles, e.g.

εὐτυχισμένος, happy
δυστυχισμένος, unhappy

Adverbs can be formed from Passive Participles in the usual manner, e.g.

χαρούμενα, gladly
μεθυσμένα, drunkenly

VOCABULARY

ντύνομαι, I get dressed
καρφώνω, I fix
συζητῶ, I discuss, argue
χαϊδεμένος, pampered, spoilt
ὁ λόγος, reason
ὁ παράδεισος, paradise
ἡ κομψότητα, smartness
τό χαμόγελο, smile
ἡ ἰδιοτροπία, caprice, whim
προσκαλῶ, I invite
χαμένος, lost
βυθίζω, I immerse

EXERCISE 42

Translate:

1. Ἦταν μεθυσμένος καί δέν ἤξερε τί ἔλεγε.
2. Σήμερα εἶμαι πολύ χαρούμενη.
3. Ἡ Ἑλένη φαινόταν συγκινημένη.
4. Ἦταν ντυμένος μέ πολλή κομψότητα.
5. Εἶχε διαρκῶς τά μάτια της καρφωμένα ἐπάνω του.
6. Ἡ κυρία Μπράουν κούνησε τό κεφάλι της μ᾿ ἕνα εὐτυχισμένο χαμόγελο.
7. Σέ μιά φωτισμένη βεράντα κάθονταν τρεῖς ἄντρες και συζητοῦσαν.
8. Ὅλα αὐτά εἶναι ἰδιοτροπίες χαϊδεμένου παιδιοῦ.

EXERCISE 43

Translate:

1. Why are you so sad?
2. He was scared.
3. We are invited to Mrs. Petrides' party.
4. I worked a lot and I am tired.
5. I do not know the reason, but I am very unhappy.
6. Milton wrote *Paradise Lost*.
7. He was immersed (*βυθισμένος*) in his thoughts.
8. I am angry with you.

ADVERBIALS

Adverbials form another class of invariable words. They are adverbs used to qualify mainly adjectives or other adverbs and they are normally put in front of the words they qualify like πολύ in these sentences:

Τό κρασί ἦταν πολύ καλό, The wine was very good.
Πῆγαν πολύ μακριά, They went very far.

The following words are adverbials as they can replace πολύ in the above or equivalent sentences:

ἀρκετά, fairly
μᾶλλον, rather
πάρα πολύ, very much
πιό, more
λίγο, rather
περισσότερο, more
λιγότερο, less
ἀκόμα, even
τόσο, so
ἔτσι, so
τρομερά, awfully
σχεδόν, almost
ἐντελῶς, completely
ὄχι, not
ὅσο, as . . . as

The above words can also precede nouns which are used in an adjectival manner, e.g.

Ὁ Κώστας εἶναι πολύ κύριος, Costas is very much a gentleman.

There is one adverbial which usually precedes nouns. This is *σά* (*σάν* in front of vowels or *κ*, *π*, *τ*, *ξ*, *ψ*), like, e.g.

Περπατοῦσε σάν ἀξιωματικός, He was walking like an officer.

VOCABULARY

ἡ θέσις, seat
ἡ περιουσία, property
ὁ καφές, coffee
ἡ χάρη, favour
ἔξυπνος, intelligent
ἀστεῖος, funny
τό φαΐ, food, meal
ἀδύνατος, weak
γλυκύς, sweet
ὁ γυιός, son
ἄγνωστος, unknown
εὐγενής, polite

EXERCISE 44

Translate:

1. *Αὐτή ἡ θέσις εἶναι πολύ μπροστά.*
2. *Μοῦ εἶναι σχεδόν ἀδύνατο νά τό πιστέψω.*
3. *Ὁ πατέρας του ἔχει μιάν ἀρκετά μεγάλη περιουσία.*
4. *Θέλω ἕνα καφέ, μᾶλλον γλυκύ.*
5. *Εἶναι τόσο δύσκολο νά μοῦ κάνεις αὐτή τή χάρη;*
6. *Ὁ γυιός σας εἶναι τρομερά ἔξυπνος.*
7. *Αὐτός ὁ ἄνθρωπος μοῦ εἶναι ἐντελῶς ἄγνωστος.*
8. *Εἶναι πάρα πολύ ἀστεῖο.*
9. *Εἶστε πολύ εὐγενής.*
10. *Αὐτό τό κρασί εἶναι ἀκόμα καλύτερο.*
11. *Θέλετε νερό; Ναί, ἀλλά ὄχι πολύ.*
12. *Αὐτό τό φαΐ εἶναι πιό καλό ἀπό ἐκεῖνο.*
13. *Δέ βλέπω πολύ μακριά.*
14. *Ξύπνησα πολύ ἀργά καί πῆγα στή δουλειά στίς δέκα ἡ ὥρα.*

INTERROGATIVE ADVERBS

There is a class of interrogative words which have certain characteristics of adverbs. They are called interrogative adverbs and are put in front of verbs as questions, such as

Πότε ἦρθε ὁ Ἀντώνης; When did Anthony come?
Ποῦ εἶναι τά σπίρτα; Where are the matches?

The following words belong to this class:

πότε; when? *μήπως;* equivalent to "I wonder if"
ποῦ; where? *ἄραγε;* equivalent to "I wonder if"
πῶς; how? *ὥστε;* so?
γιατί; why?

Μήπως and *ἄραγε* are usually associated with future events, e.g.

Μήπως θά εἶναι καί ὁ Γιάννης ἐκεῖ; Will John be there too, I wonder?
Ἄραγε θά ἔρθει; Now will he come?

Similar to the above are the interrogative adjectives *ποιός;* who, gen. *ποιανοῦ*, whose; *τί*, what, gen. *τίνος*, whose; *πόσος*, how much, e.g.

Ποιός ἦρθε; Who came?
Ποιανοῦ εἶναι τό σπίτι; Whose is the house?
Τί εἶναι αὐτό; What is this?
Τίνος εἶναι αὐτό; Whose is this?
Πόσο κάνουν οἱ πατάτες σήμερα; How much are potatoes today?

VOCABULARY

ἐμποδίζω, I stop, prevent
τίποτε, anything
σκέφτομαι, I think
τό ποδήλατο, bicycle
ἄσχημος, bad, ugly
τό πρᾶγμα, thing
φεύγω, I leave, go away

EXERCISE 45

Translate:

1. *Ποῦ θές νά πᾶς; τοῦ εἶπε ἀπότομα.*
2. *Ποιός θά μ' ἐμποδίσει;*
3. *Πόσων χρονῶν εἶσαι;*
4. *Μήπως μοῦ ἦρθες μεθυσμένος;*
5. *Ποιά εἶναι ἡ οἰκογένειά σου;*
6. *Τί σκέφτεσαι νά κάνεις;*
7. *Γιατί ρωτᾶς;*
8. *Πῶς εἶναι ὁ πατέρας σου; Πολύ καλά, εὐχαριστῶ.*
9. *Ἄραγε, θά μέ θυμηθεῖ;*
10. *Πῶς εἶστε; Ὄχι καί ἄσχημα.*
11. *Ποιανοῦ εἶναι αὐτό τό ποδήλατο;*

EXERCISE 46

Translate:

1. Why are you leaving so early?
2. What do you want to say?
3. Why not?
4. I wonder if (*μήπως*) you are hiding anything from me?
5. What could he do on his own?
6. What time is it, please?
7. So, you are leaving?
8. Do you think then, that I can wait for you for two hours?
9. Why are you telling me these (things)?

CONJUNCTIONS

Invariable words called conjunctions are used to connect two verbs belonging to two different phrases, as *ὅταν* and *ὅτι* in the following sentences:

Φύγαμε ὅταν τελείωσε τό ἔργο, We left when the play ended.
Εἶπε ὅτι τελείωσε τό ἔργο, He said that the play had ended.

The following words, which can replace *ὅταν* or *ὅτι* in the above or equivalent sentences, are termed conjunctions:

ἀφοῦ, after
σάν, as
καί, and
ἐνῶ, while
ὅμως, however
μετά, after
ἄνκαι, although
μόλις, as soon as
μολονότι, although
ἀλλά, but
ὥσπου, until
ἴσως, in the hope that, in case
γιατί, because
πώς, *πού*, that
ἐπειδή, because
καθώς, as
μήπως, lest
ὅποτε, whenever
ὅπως, as
ἄλλωστε, besides
ὅτι, that
τί, what
νά, that
ἄν, if
πρίν or *προτοῦ*, before
ὅπου, where

Most of the above conjunctions can precede verbs in almost any tense, e.g.

Τρῶμε ὅταν πεινᾶμε, We eat when we are hungry.
Φάγαμε ὅταν πεινάσαμε, We ate when we got hungry.

Θά φᾶμε ὅταν πεινάσουμε, We shall eat when we get hungry.

Some, however, are normally associated with particular tenses of the verb.

One of these conjunctions is *πρίν*, before, which usually precedes the Indefinite, e.g.

Φύγαμε πρίν τελειώσει τό ἔργο, We left before the play had ended.

The conjunction *ὅποτε* can precede the Present or the Imperfect, e.g.

Φεύγαμε ὅποτε δέ μᾶς εὐχαριστοῦσε τό ἔργο, We used to leave whenever the play did not please us.

EXAMPLES

Νομίζω πώς δέν ἔχετε δίκαιο, I think that you are not right.

Τόν ἐκτιμῶ πολύ ἄνκαι δέν τόν γνωρίζω, I respect him very much although I do not know him.

Φοβόταν μήπως τόν χάσει, He was afraid he might lose him.

Κάνε ὅπως θές, Do as you like.

'Εκεῖνος πῆγε κοντά του καί τόν χαιρέτησε, He went near him and greeted him.

Δέν ἤξερε τί νά πεῖ, He didn't know what to say.

VOCABULARY

τελειώνω, finish, end
ὁ καλλιτέχνης artist
ἡ ἀξία, worth, value
θαρρῶ, I think
καθυστερῶ, I am late
ἡ περιπέτεια, adventure
τό τραῖνο, train
ξαναβλέπω, I see again
προσέχω, I notice
μετανιώνω, I change my mind, repent

εἶναι ἀνάγκη, it is necessary
τό ἔργο, work (dramatic), play
ἰδιαίτερος, special
στενοχωρημένος, worried
τά καθέκαστα, events, details
ἀρκετά, a fair amount, enough
μαθαίνω, I learn
ξεκινῶ, I start
γερός, healthy and strong
κάτι, something
παράξενος, strange, unusual

EXERCISE 47

Translate:

1. *Φύγαμε ὅταν τελείωσε τό ἔργο.*
2. *Μιλοῦσε γιατί ἤθελε νά ξεχάσει.*
3. *Τόν θύμωσε γιατί τοῦ μίλησε ἀπότομα.*
4. *Τώρα ἔβλεπε πώς οἱ καλλιτέχνες εἶχαν μιάν ἰδιαίτερη ἀξία στή ζωή.*
5. *Βγῆκαν ἀπό τό δωμάτιο ἀφοῦ ἔσβυσαν τό φῶς.*
6. *Γελοῦσε ἐνῶ μέσα του ἦταν πολύ στενοχωρημένος.*
7. *Αὔριο ὅταν θά εἶσαι καλά, μ' εὐχαριστεῖς.*
8. *Μή θαρρεῖς πώς ντρέπομαι γι' αὐτό.*
9. *Εἶπε ὅτι θά ἐρχότανε στίς ὀκτώ.*
10. *Ὁ ἀξιωματικός δέν ἦταν ἐκεῖ ἀλλά ἤξερε ὅλα τά καθέκαστα.*
11. *Δέν νομίζεις πώς καθυστερήσαμε ἀρκετά;*
12. *Εἶχα τίς περιπέτειές μου. Νομίζω νά τίς ἔμαθες.*
13. *Περιμένω ἴσως ἔρθει.*
14. *Ἔμεινα ἐκεῖ ὥσπου ξεκίνησε τό τραῖνο.*
15. *Ἦταν εὐτυχισμένοι πού τόν ξαναεῖδαν γερό.*

EXERCISE 48

Translate:

1. He noticed that the lights were off in the house.
2. For a moment he seemed as if he wanted to say something but he changed his mind.

3. He left him after he had turned and looked at him angrily.
4. I cannot speak well but I want to say this.
5. He goes away whenever you come.
6. He used to tell us not to smoke, but he smoked a lot.
7. I stayed there until they came.
8. As I was walking in the street I saw something unusual.
9. He was afraid lest his father should leave him.
10. Do as you like.
11. Come, although it is not very necessary.
12. Go wherever you like.
13. He came as soon as he heard it.

THE USE OF *ἄν*

The conjunction *ἄν* is usually put at the beginning of a sentence to express a conditional event. When the condition refers to a future event the *ἄν* is followed by the Indefinite while the verb of the second sentence is formed by *θά* and the Indefinite or by the Imperative, e.g.

ἄν θέλεις νά πᾶς, πήγαινε, If you want to go, go.
ἄν πᾶς στό σινεμά θά δεῖς ἕνα καλό φίλμ, If you go to the cinema you will see a good film.

When the condition refers to an event in the past the *ἄν* is followed by the Imperfect while the verb of the second sentence is formed by *θά* and the Imperfect, e.g.

ἄν πήγαινες στό σινεμά χθές, θά ἔβλεπες ἕνα καλό φίλμ, If you had gone to the cinema you would have seen a good film; *or* if you went . . . you would see . . .
ἄν μέ ρωτοῦσαν θά ἔλεγα ὅτι δέν ἦταν σωστό, If I were asked I would have said (*or* I would say) that it was not right.

FURTHER CONJUNCTIONS

Some of the above conjunctions connect a noun and a sentence that refers to it. Such conjunctions are *πού*, that, who, whom, and *ὅπου*, where, e.g.

Τό βιβλίο πού διάβασα σήμερα ἦταν θαυμάσιο, The book that I read today was wonderful.

Πού may be replaced by the adjective *ὁ ὁποῖος*, e.g.

Τό βιβλίο τό ὁποῖο διάβασα σήμερα ἦταν θαυμάσιο, The book that I read today was wonderful.
Τό ἑστιατόριο ὅπου φάγαμε τό μεσημέρι ἦταν ἀπαίσιο, The restaurant where we ate at noon was horrible.

Another conjunction is *ὅ,τι*, what, which implies both a noun and *πού* and which is used in sentences such as *Εἶχε ὅ,τι ἤθελε*, He had what he wanted.

VOCABULARY

ἡ κατοχή, occupation
χρωστῶ, I owe
τό νοίκι, rent
τό πρωϊνό, morning
ὁ πλοῦτος, wealth
συχνάζω, frequent
ξαναδίνω, give back
ἀπόψε, tonight
βοηθῶ, I help
μένω, I stay
ἀπολαμβάνω, I enjoy
στεροῦμαι, I am deprived of
ἀπροσδόκητα, unexpectedly
συνήθως, usually
ἀνήκω, I belong
ἡ μουσική, music
τό καφενεῖο, café

EXERCISE 49

Translate:

1. *Εἶναι ὁ Ἄγγλος πού ἦταν ἐδῶ τόν καιρό τῆς κατοχῆς.*
2. *Ἦρθε στήν Ἑλλάδα μέ κάμποσα λεφτά πού εἶχε κάνει στήν Ἀμερική.*
3. *Αὐτή τήν ὥρα πού μιλοῦμε χρωστᾶς τό νοίκι σου.*
4. *Ἦταν κάτι πού δέν τό περίμενε.*
5. *Ἄν ἔμενε σιωπηλός δέν ἦταν γιατί δέν εἶχε τίποτε νά πεῖ.*
6. *Ἀπέναντι φαίνονταν δυό ζευγάρια πού χόρευαν.*
7. *Εἶδα τό Βάσο πού ἀπολάμβανε τό πρωϊνό στή βεράντα.*
8. *Δέν ἤθελε νά στερηθεῖ τόν πλοῦτο πού τόσο ἀπροσδόκητα τοῦ εἶχε πέσει.*
9. *Κάνε ὅ,τι θέλεις.*
10. *Πῆγε νά τόν βρεῖ στοῦ Γιάννη ὅπου σύχναζε συνήθως τά πρωϊνά.*
11. *Εἶμαι ἕνας ἄνθρωπος πού θέλει νά σοῦ ξαναδόσει τήν εὐτυχία πού ἔχασες, τόν πλοῦτο πού σοῦ ἀνήκει, τήν οἰκογένεια πού δέ χάρηκες.*

EXERCISE 50

Translate:

1. If you want to come, come tonight.
2. This is the book (that) I gave (to) you.
3. (At) the moment (when) they sat down, the music started (playing).
4. He is the man who helped us at a difficult moment.
5. He went to the café where his friends used to go.
6. We saw two women who were arguing.

CONNECTIVES

Connectives form another class of invariable words. They are conjunctions used to join together two nouns, or pronouns, or adjectives or verbs or adverbs, e.g.

Τά αὐτοκίνητα καί τά ἀεροπλάνα εἶναι χρήσιμα καί εὐχάριστα, Cars and airplanes are useful and pleasant.
Χτές καί σήμερα χορέψαμε καί τραγουδήσαμε, Yesterday and today we danced and sang.

Other connectives are: *ἤ*, or; *γιά*, or; *ἀλλά*, but.
Some connectives are repeated in front of both words that they connect, e.g.

Οὔτε ἐγώ οὔτε αὐτός θά πάει, Neither I nor he will go.

Other such connectives are: *εἴτε . . . εἴτε*, either . . . or; *ἤ . . . ἤ*, either . . . or; *ὄχι . . . ἀλλά*, not . . . but, e.g.

Εἴτε αὐτό εἴτε ἐκεῖνο, Either this one or that one.
Ὄχι αὐτό ἀλλά ἐκεῖνο. Not this one but that one.

VERBAL PARTICLES

Verbal Particles are words which precede verbs to denote time or mood or negation, etc. Such words are:

θά, νά, δέν, μή, ἄς, γιά νά.

These particles cannot be translated as they do not normally stand by themselves. Their meaning becomes apparent in their usage.

Θά, νά and *δέν* have been examined in previous chapters (see pp. 67, 88). There are, however, more uses of *θά* and *νά*, as in the following examples:

Θά πῆγε στό θέατρο, He must have gone to the theatre.
Θά εἶχε περάσει τά σαράντα, He most probably was over forty.

Thus it can be seen that *θά* with the Past or the Past Perfect denotes a very probable assumption. On the other hand *θά* with the Imperfect is equivalent to English verbs preceded by *would*, e.g.

Θά πήγαινα, I would have gone, I would go.
Θά ἤθελα ἕνα ποτήρι νερό, I would like a glass of water.

The particle *νά* followed by the Present or the Indefinite may be used in questions, and is equivalent to English *shall*, e.g.

Νά κλείσω τήν πόρτα; Shall I close the door?

When *νά* is followed by the Imperfect in questions it is equivalent to English *should*, e.g.

Νά πήγαινε ἤ νά μή πήγαινε; Should he go or should he not go?

Νά ἔλεγε πώς τό θυμόταν; Should he say that he remembered it?

When it is not a matter of interrogation the Greek equivalent of *should* is *ἔπρεπε νά*, e.g.

Ἔπρεπε νά πᾶς, You should go.
Ἔπρεπε νά πήγαινες, You should have gone.

Νά is also used in such expressions.

Νά ζεῖ κανείς (= one), *ἤ νά μή ζεῖ,* to be or not to be.

Νά is also used after *σά* to express the equivalent of *as if*, e.g.

Μιλᾶς σά νά μή θέλεις νά πᾶς, You speak as if you do not want to go.

When preceded by *μακάρι, νά** expresses the equivalent of *I wish*, etc., e.g.

Μακάρι νά μποροῦσα νά ἔρθω, I wish I could come.

Ἄς may be used with the first or third person of the Present or the Indefinite to express either continuous or non-continuous decision or desire. It is, therefore, equivalent to the Imperative for those persons, e.g.

ἄς γράφει, let him write
ἄς σηκωθῶ, let me get up
ἄς πᾶνε, let them go

Μή can be considered as the negative form of *ἄς*. It is used with the second person, e.g.

Μή τραγουδᾶτε, do not sing
Μή φύγεις, do not go

* A rare use of *νά* is in this sentence:
Ἡ ἀπάντηση δέ φάνηκε νά ἔπεισε τή μητέρα του, The answer did not seem to have convinced his mother,
where it is used as a conjunction.

It may, however, also be used with the first or third person when it is preceded by ἄς, e.g.

ἄς μή μιλήσω, I had better not speak
ἄς μή ἔρθουν, let them not come

Γιά νά is used as a substitute of *νά* to express the English equivalent of *in order to*, e.g.

Ἔμεινε στό σπίτι γιά νά διαβάσει, He stayed at home in order to read.

VOCABULARY

ὑποχρεωμένος, forced, obliged
σπουδαῖος, important
ὁπωσδήποτε, in any case
ὁ βασιλιάς, king
πίνω, I drink
τά βάσανα, troubles
εἶμαι ὑποχρεωμένος, I have to
τό τηλεφώνημα, phone-call
ἡ εὐγένεια, politeness
ξεχνῶ (Indef. *ξεχάσω*), I forget
νικῶ, I win, beat

EXERCISE 51

Translate:

1. *Δέ θέλω οὔτε νά σέ δῶ οὔτε νά μέ δεῖς.*
2. *Νά πᾶς εἴτε ἐσύ εἴτε ὁ ἀδερφός σου.*
3. *Εἶμαι ὑποχρεωμένος νά μείνω στό σπίτι ὄχι μόνο γιατί θέλω νά δουλέψω ἀλλά καί γιατί περιμένω ἕνα σπουδαῖο τηλεφώνημα.*
4. *Ὁπωσδήποτε θά ξεκίνησαν στίς τρεῖς.*
5. *Θά ξεκινούσαμε στίς τρεῖς ἄν ἐρχόσασταν στήν ὥρα σας.*
6. *Θά ἤθελα πολύ νά δῶ τό Βασιλιά Λήρ ἀπόψε.*
7. *Νά μείνω ἤ νά φύγω;*
8. *Ἔπρεπε νά μοῦ ἔγραφες μόλις πῆρες τό γράμμα μου.*

9. *Ἔπρεπε νά ἔρθεις ἀμέσως.*
10. *Μοῦ μιλοῦσε μέ πολλή εὐγένεια, σά νά μή μέ ἤξερε.*
11. *Ἄς τραγουδήσουμε ὅλοι μαζί.*
12. *Ἔπινε γιά νά ξεχάσει τά βάσανά του.*
13. *Μακάρι νά νικήσετε.*
14. *Δέ μοῦ ἀρέσει νά σηκώνομαι πολύ νωρίς.*

PREPOSITIONS

We have already used a number of prepositions. They can be defined as invariable words that precede nouns or pronouns which are in the accusative case. Thus, all words that can replace *σ'* or *γιά* in the following or equivalent sentences are prepositions:

Πῆγε σ'τήν Κρήτη, He went to Crete.
Αὐτό εἶναι γιά σένα, This is for you.

Besides *σ'* (which is also found as *σέ*) and *γιά* the most common prepositions are:

μέ, with	*σά*, like
ἀπό, from, by	*πρός*, towards
ὥς, till, up to	*πρίν*, before
μετά, after	*παρά*, in spite of, against; etc.
χωρίς, without	

A number of adverbs can precede the prepositions *σέ*, *μέ* and *ἀπό* to form complex prepositions such as:

πάνω σέ, on, upon	*ἐμπρός ἀπό*, in front of
κοντά σέ, near	*κάτω ἀπό*, beneath, below
μέσα σέ, in, into	*πίσω ἀπό*, behind
δίπλα σέ, beside	*γύρω ἀπό*, round
πλάϊ σέ, beside	*ἔξω ἀπό*, outside
γύρω σέ, round	*πρίν ἀπό*, before
μαζί μέ, together, with	*ὕστερα ἀπό*, after
πάνω ἀπό, over, above	

VOCABULARY

ἡ ἀπόφαση, decision
ἡ πετσέτα, towel, napkin
ἡ προσοχή, attention
ἡ πολυθρόνα, armchair
ὁ ἀέρας, air, wind
ἡ τσάντα, brief-case, handbag
περιποιοῦμαι, I look after
καταπληκτικά, strikingly
τό κέντρο, centre
τό διαμέρισμα, flat
τό καλάθι, basket
περισσότερος, more
ἡ φωτιά, fire
σιδηροδρομικῶς, by train
φροντίζω, I take care of
ἡ φωτογραφία, photograph
ξαπλώνομαι, I stretch myself out
φυσῶ, I blow
ἡ βιβλιοθήκη, library
τό μπράτσο, arm
μοιάζω, I resemble
τό ἀστέρι, star
κατοικῶ, I live, inhabit
ἡ πέννα, pen, penny
τό μῆλο, apple
τό βλέμμα, look, glance
τό πεζοδρόμιο, pavement
ἀεροπορικῶς, by air
ἡ γυναίκα, woman, wife

EXERCISE 52

Translate:

1. *Ἔφθασε ἡ ὥρα γιά τή μεγάλη ἀπόφαση.*
2. *Ἡ γυναίκα μου φροντίζει γιά ὅλα τά πράγματα τοῦ σπιτιοῦ.*
3. *Μέ τήν πετσέτα στό χέρι πῆγε στό παράθυρο.*
4. *Πῆρε τή φωτογραφία ἀπό τά χέρια τοῦ Κώστα, τήν κοίταξε μέ προσοχή καί τοῦ τήν ἔδωσε πίσω γελώντας.*
5. *Ξαπλώθηκε στήν πολυθρόνα ὅπου πρίν ἀπό λίγο καθόταν ὁ ἄγνωστος κύριος.*
6. *Ἀπό τή θάλασσα φυσοῦσε κρύος ἀέρας.*
7. *Θά εἶμαι στή βιβλιοθήκη ἀπό τίς δέκα τό πρωΐ ὥς τίς πέντε τό ἀπόγευμα.*
8. *Νά ἔρθετε νά μέ πάρετε μετά τίς πέντε.*

9. *Ἔσφιξε τήν τσάντα κάτω ἀπό τό μπράτσο του.*
10. *Ἔξω ἀπό τήν πόρτα περίμενε ἕνα ταξί.*
11. *Μέ περιποιόταν σά μητέρα.*
12. *Τοῦ εἶπα καλά λόγια γιά σένα.*
13. *Αὐτός ὁ ἄνθρωπος μοιάζει καταπληκτικά μέ τόν πατέρα μου.*
14. *Τόν εἶδα ὕστερα ἀπό τρία χρόνια.*

EXERCISE 53

Translate:

1. I shouldn't be able to do anything without your help.
2. He arrived at his house very late.
3. He looks like a film star.
4. He advanced towards the middle of the room.
5. My house is near the centre of the city.
6. I live in a flat with two friends of mine.
7. Your pen is on top of the wireless set.
8. The apples are inside the basket.
9. From 5 till 7 I shall be at home.
10. Her look said much more than her words.
11. The car stopped beside the pavement.
12. They all sat round the fire.
13. They started off for Piraeus.
14. He went to England by plane.
15. I shall go to Germany by air or by rail.

DETERMINERS

There is one class which contains both variable and invariable words. They are the articles and those words which, in order to determine nouns, can replace the articles *ὁ* or *οἱ* in the following or equivalent sentences:

<u>*Ὁ*</u> *ἄνθρωπος εἶναι τίμιος*, The man is honest.
<u>*Οἱ*</u> *ἄνθρωποι εἶναι τίμιοι*, The men are honest.

Determiners include articles, numerals and words like *some, most, a little, many*, etc., e.g.

Αὐτός ὁ, this
Ἕνας, μιά, ἕνα, one, a
κανένας, καμμιά, κανένα, no one, one
λίγος, a little
πολύς, much
μερικοί, some
οἱ περισσότεροι, most
ἐκεῖνος, that
ὅλος, all
κάποιος, someone
τρεῖς, three
τέσσερεις, four
διακόσιοι,* two hundred
τριακόσιοι, three hundred
χίλιοι, one thousand, etc.

The invariable words of this class are:

κάθε, every
κάτι, something, some

Numerals can be either invariable or variable, e.g.

Invariable:	*πέντε*,	5
	τριάντα ὀκτώ,	38
	ἑκατό	100
Variable:	*ἕνα*,	1
	διακόσια,	200

* Note that *διακόσιοι, διακόσιες, διακόσια*, etc. are adjectivals.

Variable:	τριακόσια,	300
	τετρακόσια,	400
	πεντακόσια,	500
	ἑξακόσια,	600
	ἑπτακόσια,	700
	ὀκτακόσια,	800
	ἐννιακόσια,	900
	χίλια,	1,000

Numerals may also be partly variable, e.g.

τετρακόσια πενήντα ἕξι, 456
ἕνα ἑκατομμύριο, 1,000,000
ἕνα ἑκατομμύριο πεντακόσιες χιλιάδες ὀχτακόσια τριάντα τέσσερα, 1,500,834

VOCABULARY

ἀνήσυχος, restless
ὁ Σπαρτιάτης, Spartan
οἱ Θερμοπύλες, Thermopylae
ὁ βλάκας, stupid man, fool
ὁ καιρός, time, weather
τό σελίνι, shilling
ὁ πόλεμος, war
ὁ κόσμος, world, people
πολεμῶ, I fight
γυρεύω, I look for
τά χαρτιά, cards
ἀπίθανος, improbable
ἡ πέννα, penny
τελειώνω, I finish

EXERCISE 54

Translate:

1. *Ὅλος ὁ κόσμος εἶναι ἀνήσυχος.*
2. *Μερικές μέρες εἶναι πολύ ζεστές καί μερικές εἶναι πολύ κρύες.*
3. *Τριακόσιοι Σπαρτιᾶτες κάτω ἀπό τό Λεωνίδα πολεμήσανε στίς Θερμοπύλες.*

4. *Κάποιος κύριος ἦρθε καί σᾶς γύρευε.*
5. *Οἱ περισσότεροι ἄνθρωποι δέν εἶναι οὔτε βλάκες οὔτε ἔξυπνοι.*
6. *Ἔχασε χίλιες λίρες στά χαρτιά.*
7. *Κάθε πράγμα στόν καιρό του.*
8. *Πολλοί ἐργάτες εἶναι χωρίς δουλειά.*
9. *Μοῦ εἶπε κάτι πολύ ἀπίθανο.*
10. *Ξόδεψα τετρακόσιες τριάντα ὀκτώ λίρες δώδεκα σελίνια καί ὀκτὼ πέννες.*
11. *Ὁ τελευταῖος πόλεμος ἄρχισε τό χίλια ἐννιακόσια τριάντα ἐννιά καί τελειωσε τό χίλια ἐννιακόσια σαράντα πέντε.*

EXERCISE 55

Write in full:

(*a*) 1,743. (*b*) 634. (*c*) 42,770. (*d*) 10,500. (*e*) 836,124. (*f*) 406. (*g*) 23,205. (*h*) 1,376,228.

SUFFIXES

The ending or suffix of the nominative case of nouns may indicate both gender and general meaning. No hard and fast rules can be given for the significance of suffixes but the following important ones may be noticed:

M nouns:

-*τζῆς*, denoting mostly jobs, e.g. *ὁ καφετζῆς*, café proprietor.
-*ισμός*, corresponding to English *-ism*, e.g. *ὁ σοσιαλισμός*, socialism.
-*ᾶς*, denoting mostly jobs, e.g. *ὁ γαλατᾶς*, milkman.
-*τής*, denoting the performer of an action, e.g. *ὁ παρατηρητής*, observer.
-*αῖος*, a mostly ethnic suffix, e.g. *ὁ Ἀθηναῖος*, Athenian; *Ἑβραῖος*, Hebrew, Jew.
-*έζος*, mostly ethnic, e.g. *ὁ Ἐγγλέζος*, Englishman; *Κινέζος*, Chinese.

F nouns:

-*ισσα*, ethnic and andronymic suffix, e.g. *ἡ Σπαρτιάτισσα*, Spartan woman; *ἡ Βασίλισσα*, Queen.
-*τητα*, denoting quality, e.g. *ἡ ὡραιότητα*, beauty.
-*άδα*, e.g. *ἡ πορτοκαλλάδα*, orangeade.
-*ίδα*, mostly ethnic, e.g. *ἡ Ἀγγλίδα*, Englishwoman; *ἡ Γερμανίδα*, German woman.
-*αινα*, mostly denoting female sex, e.g. *ἡ Κώσταινα*, Mrs. Costas; *ἡ γιάτραινα*, woman doctor, or the wife of the doctor.
-*αριά*, *ἡ ζυγαριά*, balance; *δεκαριά*, approximately ten (objects) together.

-*σύνη*, mostly denoting a quality, e.g. *ἡ καλωσύνη*, goodness, kindness.
-*τρια*, F suffix corresponding to an M suffix in -*τής*, e.g. *μαθητής*, pupil (masc.); *μαθήτρια*, pupil (fem.).

N nouns:
-*ιμο*, mostly denoting an action, e.g. *τό πλύσιμο*, washing.
-*άδι*, e.g. *τό πετράδι*, gem; *τό σκοτάδι*, darkness.
-*μα*, mostly denoting an action, e.g. *τό κάπνισμα*, smoking.
-*τήρι*, mostly denoting an instrument, e.g. *ξυπνητήρι*, alarm clock.

The most usual suffixes of adjectives are the following:

-*άτικος*, e.g. *Κυριακάτικος*, Sunday (adj.).
-*ᾶτος*, e.g. *γεμᾶτος*, full.
-*ιάρης*, having a rather pejorative sense, e.g. *ζηλιάρης*, jealous.
-*ικός*, e.g. *ἀδελφικός*, brotherly.
-*ινός*, e.g. *χειμερινός*, wintry.
ωπός, mostly corresponding to the English suffix -*ish*, e.g. *κοκκινωπός*, reddish.
-*ερός*, e.g. *βροχερός*, rainy.
-*ητικός*, e.g. *συγκινητικός*, moving.
-*ουλλός*, also similar to -*ish*, e.g. *παχουλλός*, rather fat.
-*ωτός*, e.g. *ὀδοντωτός*, serrated.
-*πλός*, added to numerals, e.g. *διπλός*, double; *τριπλός*, treble.
-*πλάσιος*, added to numerals, e.g. *διπλάσιος*, twice as big; *πενταπλάσιος*, five times as big.
-*ούτσικος*, a diminutive suffix, e.g. *καλούτσικος*, quite good.

The diminutive suffixes for nouns are the following:

M nouns:
-*ούλης*, e.g. *ἀδερφούλης*, brother.

F nouns:
-*ιτσα*, e.g. *σαλατίτσα*, salad.
-*ούλα*, e.g. *ἀδερφούλα*, sister.
-*πούλα*, e.g. *βοσκοπούλα*, shepherdess.
-*ούδα*, e.g. *κοπελλούδα*, young girl.

N nouns:
-*άκι*, e.g. *τραπεζάκι*, small table.
-*ούδι*, e.g. *ἀγγελούδι*, little angel.
-*πουλο*, e.g. *βασιλόπουλο*, young prince.

The augmentative suffixes are the following:

M nouns:
-*αρᾶς*, e.g. *ψευταρᾶς*, big liar.
-*αρος*, e.g. *ψεύταρος*, big liar.

F nouns:
-*άρα*, e.g. *ποδάρα*, big foot.

COMBINATION OF WORDS

The combination of two or more words to form a compound is a common feature of the Greek language. Almost any part of speech can be used for such combinations but the main types of compound words consist of:

1. Two nouns, e.g.

   Σάββατο-Κυριακή = *τό σαββατοκυριακο*, weekend
   ἄντρας-γυναίκα = *τό ἀντρόγυνο*, couple
   μαχαίρι-πηρούνι = *τά μαχαιροπήρουνα*, knives and forks, cutlery

2. An adjective* or other word and a noun, e.g.

   πρῶτο-μάστορας = *ὁ πρωτομάστορας*, master craftsman
   φίλο-λόγος = *ὁ φιλόλογος*, philologist
   παλιο-ἄνθρωπος = *ὁ παλιάνθρωπος*, rascal
   ἀρχι-τελώνης = *ὁ ἀρχιτελώνης*, chief customs officer

3. Almost any kind of word and an adjective, e.g.

   όλο-ἄσπρος = *ολόασπρος*, all white
   πολυ-μαθής = *πολυμαθής*, learned
   κατά-μαῦρος = *κατάμαυρος*, jet black
   προ-πολεμικός = *προπολεμικός*, pre-war
   ἀντι-παθητικός = *ἀντιπαθητικός*, unlikeable
   ὑπέρ-κομψός = *ὑπέρκομψος*, most elegant
   μισό-κλειστός = *μισόκλειστος*, half-closed

Many adjectives may also take the negative prefix *α-* (or *αν-* in front of vowels), e.g.

ἀ-γνωστός = *ἄγνωστος*, unknown
ἀν-ήσυχος = *ἀνήσυχος*, restless

* The adjective is usually in the N form.

Two verbs together, e.g.

ἀνοίγω-κλείω = *ἀνοιγοκλείω*, I open and close
πηγαίνω-ἔρχομαι = *πηγαινοέρχομαι*, I come and go

Almost any kind of word and a verb, e.g.

κρυφά-μιλῶ = *κρυφομιλῶ*, I talk quietly, whisper
γλυκά-φιλῶ = *γλυκοφιλῶ*, I kiss sweetly
χάμω-γελῶ = *χαμογελῶ*, I smile (lit. I laugh low)
ξανά-δίνω = *ξαναδίνω*, I give back, I give again
ξανά-διαβάζω = *ξαναδιαβάζω*, I re-read
καλῶς-ορίζω = *καλωσορίζω*, I welcome
στενά-χωρῶ = *στενοχωρῶ*, I vex, worry
ἀνά-βαίνω = *ἀνεβαίνω*, I go up, ascend
κατά-βαίνω = *κατεβαίνω*, I go down, descend
ἀντι-δρῶ = *ἀντιδρῶ*, I react

IDIOMS

Idioms constitute a feature of all languages. For our purpose Greek idioms may be broadly divided into two classes:

1. Real idioms, i.e. those which do not conform to the general patterns of the language. They are mainly due to the lingering of older forms of the language or to the influence of foreign languages. Such idioms are the following:

ἐν τάξει, all right
ἐν πάσῃ περιπτώσει, in any case
παραδείγματος χάριν, for example
φέρ' εἰπεῖν, for example
ἐξ ἴσου, equally
ἐν μέρει, partly
ἐν τούτοις, in spite of
κατά τά ἄλλα, in other respects
ἐκ μέρους σου, on your behalf
ἐξ ἄλλου, besides
εἰ δ' ἄλλως, otherwise, or else
στό κάτω τῆς γραφῆς, after all
ὅσον ἀφορᾶ ἐμέ, as far as I am concerned
ἔχω ὑπ' ὄψῃ μου, I take into account
πρό παντός, above all
ὅλως διόλου, completely
πέραν πάσης ἀμφιβολίας, beyond all doubt

2. Apparent idioms, i.e. those which, although conforming to the general patterns of the language, sound peculiar to English-speaking people. A considerable part of the language is idiomatic in this respect, and only a few such idioms can be given here. But a knowledge and command of them is absolutely essential to anyone wishing to know the language properly:

τά κατάφερε, he managed it
τά ἔχασε, he got confused, embarrassed
τό ἔστρωσε στό φαΐ, he tucked in to the food
τἄκανε θάλασσα, he made a mess of it
μοῦ ἀρέσει, I like
ἔχω δίκαιο, I am right
τί ἔχεις; what is the matter with you?
ἐδῶ πού τά λέμε, by the way, now we are on the subject
χωρίς ἄλλο, without fail
κόψε το, cut it out
ἄστα αὐτά, don't give me that
καί βέβαια, of course
δέν εἶμαι δά καί βλάκας, I am not a fool
ἀμέ, τί νόμισες; Yes, what did you think?
κάνει κρύο, it is cold
πρόκειται νά πάω, I am to go, I shall go
μ' ὅλο πού ἤξεραν, although they knew
ποτέ μου, never in my life
ὅλοι τους, all of them
ἔτσι κι' ἀλλιῶς, in any case
ἔτσι καί ἔτσι, so-so
πρῶτα-πρῶτα, first of all
κάνετε γρήγορα, be quick
κάθε ἄλλο, on the contrary
δέ βαρειέσαι, never mind, who cares, bother!
δέν πειράζει, it doesn't matter
θά πᾶμε πού θά πᾶμε, we shall go in any case
λοιπόν, τί θά κάνουμε; well, what shall we do?

GENERAL EXERCISES

VOCABULARY

Τί γίνεστε; How are you?
ὁ ἴδιος, same
συμφωνῶ, I agree
ἐρχόμενος, next
τίς προάλλες, the other day
ἀντίο, good-bye
ἡ ἡσυχία, quiet
τό κρῖμα, pity
πληρέστατα, most completely
ἡ ἄδεια, leave
ὁ χαιρετισμός, greeting

EXERCISE 56

A Meeting in the Street

Translate:

Καλημέρα σας.
Τί γίνεστε;
Πολύ καλά, εὐχαριστῶ, ἐσεῖς;
Τά ἴδια.
Πῶς πάει ἡ δουλειά;
Ἡσυχία.
Εἶναι κρῖμα νά δουλεύει κανείς μ' ἕνα τόσο θαυμάσιο καιρό.
Συμφωνῶ πληρέστατα.
Τήν ἐρχόμενη ἑβδομάδα ὅμως ἔχουμε δυό μέρες ἄδεια.
Τί γίνεται ὁ ἀδέλφός σας;
Καλά εἶναι. Τίς προάλλες μέ ρωτοῦσε γιά σένα.
Νά τοῦ δόσεις πολλούς χαιρετισμούς. Ἀντίο.

VOCABULARY

ἑπόμενος, next
συνοδεύω, I accompany
προσπαθῶ, I try
ἰδιαιτέρως, especially
περνῶ, I pass
βέβαιος, certain
σκοπεύω, I intend
τά καταφέρνω, I manage
τό νησί, island
κανονίζω, I fix, arrange
ὑπόσχομαι, I promise

EXERCISE 57

A Trip to the Islands

Translate:

Τήν ἑπόμενη ἑβδομάδα σκοπεύω νά πάω ταξίδι στή Μύκονο γιά λίγες μέρες. Θἄθελες νά μέ συνοδέψεις;
Θἄθελα πολύ ἀλλά δέν ξέρω ἄν θά τά καταφέρω.
Θά προσπαθήσω ὅμως καί θά σοῦ πῶ αὔριο.
Μ'ἀρέσουν πολύ τά νησιά τοῦ Αἰγαίου καί ἰδιαιτέρως ἡ Μύκονος.
Προσπάθησε νά τά κανονίσεις νά ἔρθεις καί θά περάσουμε θαυμάσια.
Δέ σοῦ ὑπόσχομαι, ἀλλά νομίζω πώς εἶναι σχεδόν βέβαιο ὅτι θά ἔρθω.

VOCABULARY

κανένας, no one, one, some	*παίζω*, I play
δοκιμάζω, I try	*ἀποφασίζω*, I decide

EXERCISE 58

An Evening Out

Translate:

Ποῦ θά πᾶμε ἀπόψε; Νά πᾶμε σινεμά, θέατρο ἤ σέ κανένα χορό;
Νομίζω πώς ἔχει ἕνα καλό φίλμ στό Παλλάς.
Παίζει ὁ Λόρενς 'Ολίβιε καί ἡ Τζήν Σίμμονς.
Μήπως εἶναι ὁ Ἄμλετ τοῦ Σαίξπηρ;
Ναί, αὐτό εἶναι.
Νομίζεις πώς θά βροῦμε θέσεις εὔκολα;
Δοκιμάζουμε κι' ἄν δέ βροῦμε θέσεις πᾶμε σέ κανένα χορό.
Ἤ μήπως θἄθελες νά πᾶμε νά φᾶμε καί νά πιοῦμε στήν Πλάκα;
Ὅπως νομίζεις. Τό ἀφίνω σέ σένα. Τηλεφώνα μου ὅμως τί ἀποφάσισες στίς πέντε τό ἀπόγευμα.

VOCABULARY

Ἀχιλλεύς, gen. *Ἀχιλλέως*, Achilles
ὁλόϊσια, straight
στρίβω, I turn
ὁ ἀστυφύλακας, policeman
ἐν τάξει, all right
τό στρίψιμο, turning
δυσκολεύομαι, I find difficulty
ἡ γωνιά, corner

EXERCISE 59

Asking the Way

Translate:

Θέλω νά πάω στήν ὁδό Ἀχιλλέως, ἀλλά ξέχασα τό δρόμο. Μπορεῖτε, σᾶς παρακαλῶ, νά μοῦ δείξετε τό δρόμο;
Νά πᾶς ὁλόϊσια καί στό τρίτο στρίψιμο νά στρίψεις ἀριστερά. Μετά νά πάρεις τό δεύτερο στρίψιμο δεξιά καί θά βρεθεῖς στήν ὁδό Ἀχιλλέως.
Εὐχαριστῶ πολύ.
Ἄν δυσκολευτεῖς, ρώτησε τόν ἀστυφύλακα πού στέκεται στή γωνιά τοῦ δρόμου.
Ἐν τάξει. Νομίζω ὅμως πώς θά τόν βρῶ χωρίς καμμιά δυσκολία.

VOCABULARY

ἐμπρός, hallo
ἀναφέρω, I mention
ἀλό, hallo
ἀκριβῶς, just
ὑπόχρεος, obliged
ἡ ὑπόθεση, matter
διαθέσιμος, available
τυχερός, lucky
ἡ διεύθυνση, address
περίφημος, wonderful

EXERCISE 60

Finding a Flat

Translate:

Μπορῶ νά μιλήσω στόν κ. Ἀλέκο παρακαλῶ;
Ἕνα λεπτό, παρακαλῶ.
Ἐμπρός.
Ὁ κ. Ἀλέκος;
Ὁ ἴδιος.
Ὁ κ. Πάνος ἐδῶ. Εἶναι γιά τήν ὑπόθεση τοῦ διαμερίσματος πού σᾶς ἀνάφερα τίς προάλλες. Μήπως ἔχετε κανένα διαθέσιμο τώρα.
Μιά στιγμή νά κοιτάξω, κ. Πάνο. Ἀλό. Εἶστε πολύ τυχερός, κ. Πάνο. Ἔχω ἀκριβῶς ἕνα πού σᾶς κάνει περίφημα. Πότε μπορεῖτε νά τό δεῖτε;
Μπορῶ σήμερα ἤ αὔριο, ἀλλά μετά τίς ἕξι.
Ἐν τάξει. Θά σᾶς δόσω τή διεύθυνση καί μπορεῖτε νά πᾶτε καί μόνος σας.
Εὐχαριστῶ πολύ. Σᾶς εἶμαι πολύ ὑπόχρεος.
Εγώ, εὐχαριστῶ.

VOCABULARY

χαλῶ, I change
εὐχαρίστως, with pleasure
τό πρακτορεῖο, agency
ἀνοιχτός, open
ἐξαργυρώνω, I cash, change
τό χαρτονόμισμα, note
περίπου, about
ἡ πληροφορία, information
Ἀγγλικός, English
τουριστικός, tourist
ἡ Τράπεζα, Bank
τό καλοκαίρι, summer
ξένος, foreign, guest
χρυσός, golden
χάρτινος, made of paper
γειά, good-bye

EXERCISE 61

Changing Money

Translate:

Μπορεῖτε σᾶς παρακαλῶ νά μοῦ πεῖτε ποῦ μπορῶ νά χαλάσω μερικές Ἀγγλικές λίρες;
Εὐχαρίστως. Νά πᾶτε σέ κανένα τουριστικό πρακτορεῖο ἢ σέ καμμιά Τράπεζα.
Ὡς ποιά ὥρα εἶναι ἀνοιχτές οἱ Τράπεζες τό καλοκαίρι;
Ὡς τίς τρεῖς τό ἀπόγευμα. Νά, ἐκεῖ κάτω εἶναι ἡ Τράπεζα τῆς Ἑλλάδος. Ἐκεῖ μπορεῖτε νά ἐξαργυρώσετε ὅλα τά ξένα χαρτονομίσματα.
Ξέρετε πόσο πάει ἡ λίρα αὐτές τίς μέρες;
Ἡ χρυσῆ λίρα πάει περίπου τριακόσιες δραχμές, καί ἡ χάρτινη περίπου ὀγδόντα τέσσερεις.
Εὐχαριστῶ πολύ γιά τίς πληροφορίες. Γειά σας.

VOCABULARY

τό ἑστιατόριο, restaurant
τό Πανεπιστήμιο, University
ὁ κατάλογος, list
ὁρίστε, here you are
ὁ φοῦρνος, oven
ἡ σαλατίτσα, salad
ἡ ρετσίνα, retsina
ἡ Ὁμόνοια, Concord
τό τρόλλεϋ, trolley-bus
στοιχίζω, I cost
μονός, single
εὐχαριστημένος, pleased
βολικός, convenient
ὁ λογαριασμός, bill
ἡ ὁδός, street
ἀκριβός, expensive
τό φαγητό, meal
τό ἀρνάκι, lamb
ἡ μερίδα, portion
ἡ μπουκάλα, bottle
συναντιέμαι, I meet
τό ξενοδοχεῖο, hotel
ἡ καθαριότης, cleanliness
πληρώνω, I pay
τό πρόγευμα, breakfast
μᾶλλον, rather
τό γκαρσόν, waiter
τά ρέστα, change

EXERCISE 62

At the Restaurant

Translate:

Ποῦ ἔχει ἕνα καλό ἑστιατόριο;
Στήν ὁδό Πανεπιστημίου.
Εἶναι ἀκριβό;
Ἔτσι κι' ἔτσι.
Μοῦ δίνετε ἕνα κατάλογο φαγητῶν, παρακαλῶ.
Ὁρίστε, κύριε. Ἔχω θαυμάσιο ἀρνάκι τοῦ φούρνου.
Ὡραῖα. Φέρε μας δυό μερίδες μέ σαλατίτσα καί νερό κρύο
Θέλετε καί κρασί;
Ναί, μιά μπουκάλα ρετσίνα.
Λοιπόν, πότε θά πᾶμε νά δοῦμε τήν Ἀκρόπολη;
Ἄν θέλεις, πᾶμε τό ἀπόγευμα.
Ἐν τάξει, τί ὥρα;

Στίς τρεῖς καί μισή.
Ποῦ θά συναντηθοῦμε;
Στήν Ὁμόνοια, ἔξω ἀπό τό ξενοδοχεῖο Αὔρα.
Μένεις ἐκεῖ κοντά;
Ὄχι, μένω μέ φίλους στήν Κυψέλη, μά εἶναι μόνο μερικά λεπτά μέ τό τρόλλεϋ. Ἐσύ μένεις κοντά στήν Ὁμόνοια;
Ναί, μένω σ'ἕνα μικρό ξενοδοχεῖο πού λέγεται "Ἡ Καθαριότης".
Πόσα σοῦ στοιχίζει;
Πληρώνω 40 δραχμές γιά ἕνα μονό δωμάτιο καί πρόγευμα.
Εἶσαι εὐχαριστημένος;
Μᾶλλον. Ἐξ ἄλλου μοῦ εἶναι ἀρκετά βολικό γιατί εἶναι στό κέντρο τῆς πόλεως.
Γκαρσόν, Πόσα ἔχουμε νά πληρώσουμε;
Ἀμέσως. Θά σᾶς φέρω τό λογαριασμό. 64 δραχμές. Ὁρίστε τά ρέστα σας.
Εὐχαριστῶ πολύ.
Σᾶς ἄρεσε τό φαγητό;
Ναί, ἦταν περίφημο.

VOCABULARY

ὁ Αὔγουστος, August
ἡ ἐκδρομή, excursion
τό πιοτό, drink
τό λεωφορεῖο, bus
καθιστός, sitting
μαχαιροπήρουνα, knives and forks
ἡ διαδρομή, trip
ἡ ἀμμουδιά, sandy beach
προτιμάω, I prefer
πυκνός, thick
ὁ γιαλός, sea-shore
μαγευτικός, delightful
ὁ οὐρανος, sky
τό κρύσταλλο, crystal
θαλασσινός, of the sea
ἡ ἡλιοθεραπεία, sun-bathing
στρώνω, spread
λείπω, I am away
ἀπαραίτητος, indispensable
ἡ ἐποχή, season
ἡ κουβέρτα, blanket
ἀκολουθῶ, I follow
τό φεγγάρι, moon
ἡ Παναγία, Virgin Mary
τό βουνό, mountain
τό πιάτο, plate
ὁ συνωστισμός, crowding
ὄρθιος, standing
πειράζει, it matters
ἀπέχει, is distant
σκιερός, shaded
φυσικά, naturally
τό πεῦκο, pine-tree
τό μαγιό, swimming-costume
γαλάζιος, blue
διάφανος, transparent
κολυμπῶ, I swim
τό παιχνίδι, game
ἡ ταβέρνα, tavern, pub
τό φαΐ (pl. τά φαγιά), food
παγωμένος, iced
τό φροῦτο, fruit
τό φαγοπότι, eating and drinking
ὁ ὕπνος, sleep
τό μπάνιο, bath, bathe
ἀπολαμβάνω, enjoy
ψόφιος, dead
ὁ γυρισμός, return
τό γέλιο, laughter
ἡ κούραση, fatigue
συνοδεύομαι, I am accompanied
τό τραγούδι, song

EXERCISE 63

A Day by the Sea

Translate:

Στίς δεκαπέντε Αὐγούστου, πού εἶναι τῆς Παναγίας, ὅλοι πᾶνε ἐκδρομή στή θάλασσα ἤ στό βουνό. Ἐκείνη τή μέρα ξυπνᾶνε πολύ πρωΐ, ἑτοιμάζουν φαγητά καί πιοτά καί τά βάζουν σέ μεγάλα καλάθια, μαζί μέ ποτήρια, πιάτα καί μαχαιροπήρουνα. Ἄλλοι πηγαίνουν μέ ἰδιωτικά αὐτοκίνητα, ἄλλοι μέ λεωφορεῖα. Ἐπειδή ὑπάρχει πολύς κόσμος, γίνεται παντοῦ μεγάλος συνωστισμός γιά νά βροῦν θέσεις. Πολλοί δέν πρόκειται νά πᾶνε καθιστοί ἀλλά ὄρθιοι. Δέν πειράζει ὅμως, ἀφοῦ ἡ διαδρομή δέν εἶναι μεγάλη.

Ἡ θάλασσα δέν ἀπέχει πολύ, καί ὅσοι πᾶνε ἐκεῖ θά βροῦν μιάν ὡραία ἀμμουδιά. Πρώτη τους δουλειά εἶναι νά ψάξουν νά βροῦν ἕνα σκιερό μέρος. Ὁ καθένας προτιμάει φυσικά ἕνα μεγάλο καί πυκνό πεῦκο κοντά στό γιαλό. Οἱ νέοι βάζουν ἀμέσως τά μαγιό τους καί πέφτουν στό νερό. Ἡ θάλασσα τῆς Ἑλλάδας εἶναι μαγευτική, γαλάζια σάν τόν οὐρανό της, καί καθαρή καί διάφανη σάν κρύσταλλο. Κολυμπᾶνε, παίζουν θαλασσινά παιχνίδια καί κάνουν ἡλιοθεραπεία μέ τίς ὧρες.

Τό μεσημέρι μερικοί τρῶνε σέ ταβέρνες. Μά οἱ περισσότεροι τό στρώνουν κάτω, καί τρῶνε τά φαγιά πού ἔχουν φέρει μαζί τους. Δέν λείπει οὔτε τό κρασί οὔτε ἡ παγωμένη μπύρα. Ἀπαραίτητα εἶναι καί τά φροῦτα τῆς ἐποχῆς. Ὕστερα ἀπό τό φαγοπότι, στρώνουν τίς κουβέρτες τους καί τό ρίχνουν στόν ὕπνο. Τό ἀπόγευμα ἀκολουθεῖ ἄλλο μπάνιο καί ἄλλο φαγοπότι, καί ὅταν ἔχει φεγγάρι μένουν ὡς ἀργά γιά νά τό ἀπολαύσουν. Ἄν καί ὅλοι εἶναι ψόφιοι στήν κούραση, ὁ γυρισμός στό σπίτι συνοδεύεται μέ γέλια καί τραγούδια.

VOCABULARY

ἅμα, when, as soon as
ἀπομένω, I stay
βαρύς, heavy, serious
βορινός, northern
ἡ γλῶσσα, tongue
ὁ θρύλος, legend
κανονικός, regular
τό καράβι, boat, ship
ὁ λιμένας, port
μακρινός, distant
μονολογῶ, I talk to myself
τό τσιμπούκι, pipe
φορτηγός, cargo (adj.)
χωμάτινος, clay (adj.)
Νορβηγός, Norwegian
ξάφνου, suddenly
ξεπροβοδίζω, I see off
ὁλόκληρος, entire
ὁ πιλότος, pilot
ἡ πορεία, course, passage
παλιός, old
τό πλοῖο, ship
ὁ πλοίαρχος, captain
ἡ πιλοτίνα, pilot-boat
συλλογίζομαι, I think
συλλογισμένος, thoughtful
τό στῆθος, chest
σταυρωμένος, crossed

EXERCISE 64

Translate:

Ὁ πιλότος Νάγκελ

Ὁ Νάγκελ Χάρμπορ, Νορβηγός πιλότος στό Κολόμπο
ἅμα ἔδινε κανονική πορεία στά καράβια
πού φεῦγαν γιά τούς ἄγνωστους καί μακρινούς λιμένες
κατέβαινε στή βάρκα του βαρύς, συλλογισμένος,
μέ τά χοντρά τά χέρια του στό στῆθος σταυρωμένα,
καπνίζοντας ἕνα παλιό χωμάτινο τσιμπούκι,
καί σέ μιά γλῶσσα βορινή σιγά μονολογώντας
ἔφευγε μόλις χάνονταν ὁλότελα τά πλοῖα.

Ὁ Νάγκελ Χάρμπορ, πλοίαρχος μέ φορτηγά καράβια,
ἀφοῦ τόν κόσμο γύρισεν ὁλόκληρο, μιά μέρα
κουράστηκε κι᾽ ἀπόμεινε πιλότος στό Κολόμπο.

Μά πάντα συλλογίζονταν τή μακρινή του χώρα
καί τά νησιά πούναι γεμάτα θρύλους—τά Λοφοῦτεν.
Καί κάποια μέρα ἐπέθανε στή πιλοτίνα μέσα
ξάφνου σάν ξεπροβόδισε τό στήμερ τάνκ Φιόρτ Φόλτεν
ὅπου ἔφευγε καπνίζοντας γιά τά νησιά Λοφοῦτεν.

Ν. ΚΑΒΒΑΔΙΑΣ

VOCABULARY

ἀμίλητος, speechless
ἀπάνω, on
ὁ δεκανέας, corporal
ἐπ' ὤμου, slope arms
καμαρωτά, jauntily
κάν, even
κύρ, Mister (familiar)
ὁ λάκκος, hole
μουρμουρίζω, I murmur
φαντάρος, soldier
μά, but
τό νοσοκομεῖο, hospital
νοσταλγικός, nostalgic
ὅλο, all the time
πέρα, beyond
πρᾶος, meek
τό ποδάρι, foot
ὁ στρατιώτης, soldier
τό σημεῖο, point
σκεπάζω, I cover
ὁ φουκαράκος, poor chap
τό χωριό, village

EXERCISE 65

Translate:

Ὁ Μιχαλιός

Τό Μιχαλιό τόν πήρανε στρατιώτη,
Καμαρωτά ξεκίνησε κι' ὡραῖα
μέ τό Μαρῆ καί μέ τόν Παναγιώτη.
Δέ μπόρεσε νά μάθει κάν τό " ἐπ' ὤμου "
Ὅλο ἐμουρμούριζε· " Κύρ-Δεκανέα,
ἄσε με νά γυρίσω στό χωριό μου."

Τόν ἄλλο χρόνο, στό νοσοκομεῖο,
ἀμίλητος τόν οὐρανό κοιτοῦσε.

'Εκάρφωνε πέρα, σ' ένα σημεῖο,
τό βλέμμα του νοσταλγικό καί πράο,
σά νάλεγε, σά νά παρακαλοῦσε·
" 'Αφῆστε με στό σπίτι μου νά πάω."

Κι' ὁ Μιχαλιός ἐπέθανε στρατιώτης.
Τόν ξεπροβόδισαν κάτι φαντάροι
μαζί τους ὁ Μαρῆς κι' ὁ Παναγιώτης.
'Απάνω του σκεπάστηκεν ὁ λάκκος
μά τοῦ ἄφησαν ἀπ' ἔξω τό ποδάρι·
'Ηταν λίγο μακρύς ὁ φουκαράκος.

Κ. ΚΑΡΥΤΑΩΚΗΣ

VOCABULARY

'Αλεξανδρινός, Alexandrian
τό ἀδέρφι, brother
ἡ ἀνθοδέσμη, bunch of flowers
ὁ ἀμέθυστος, amethyst
ἀνοιχτός, open, light (colour)
ὁ αὐλικός, courtier
αἰγυπτιακός, Egyptian
ἀξίζω, I am worth
βέβαια, of course
ἡ βασιλεία, kingdom
τό γυμνάσιο, gymnasium
τό γαλάζιο, blue colour
γοητευμένος, charmed
διπλός, double
δεμένος, tied
ἐμπροστά, in front
ἐμορφιά, beauty
ἐνθουσιάζομαι, I get enthusiastic
ἐπευφημῶ, I cheer
ἑλληνικά, Greek
ἑβραΐκα, Hebrew
ἡ ἑορτή, festivity
ἡ φορά, time
ἡ ζώνη, belt
θεατρικός, theatrical
τό θέαμα, spectacle
κηρύττω, I declare
ἡ κορδέλλα, ribbon
κεντημένος, embroidered
τό κατόρθωμα, feat
κούφιος, empty

μαζεύομαι, I gather
τό μετάξι, silk
τό μαργαριτάρι, pearl
νιώθω, I understand
ἡ παράταξις, parade
τά ποδήματα, shoes
πιότερο, more
ποιητικός, poetical
ἡ πολυτέλεια, luxury
ροδόχρους,* pink
ἡ σειρά, row
τριανταφυλλί, rose-coloured
ὁ ὑάκινθος, hyacinth
ἡ χάρις, charm

EXERCISE 66

Translate:

Ἀλεξανδρινοί βασιλεῖς

Μαζεύθηκαν οἱ Ἀλεξανδρινοί,
νά δοῦν τῆς Κλεοπάτρας τά παιδιά,
τόν Καισαρίωνα καί τά μικρά του ἀδέρφια,
Ἀλέξανδρο καί Πτολεμαῖο, πού πρώτη
φορά τά βγάζαν ἔξω στό Γυμνάσιο
ἐκεῖ νά τά κηρύξουν βασιλεῖς
μές στή λαμπρή παράταξη τῶν στρατιωτῶν.

Ὁ Ἀλέξανδρος—τόν εἶπαν βασιλέα
τῆς Ἀρμενίας, τῆς Μηδίας καί τῶν Πάρθων.
Ὁ Πτολεμαῖος—τόν εἶπαν βασιλέα
τῆς Κιλικίας, τῆς Συρίας καί τῆς Φοινίκης.
Ὁ Καισαρίων στέκονταν πιό ἐμπροστά,
ντυμένος σέ μετάξι τριανταφυλλί
στό στῆθος του ἀνθοδέσμη ἀπό ὑακίνθους,
ἡ ζώνη του διπλῆ σειρά σαπφείρων κι' ἀμεθύστων·
δεμένα τά ποδήματα του μ' ἄσπρες
κορδέλες κεντημένες μέ ροδόχροα μαργαριτάρια.
Αὐτόν τόν εἶπαν πιότερο ἀπό τούς μικρούς,
αὐτόν τόν εἶπαν Βασιλέα τῶν Βασιλέων.

* ροδόχρους is a *katharévousa* form. The following passage contains a number of such forms but they should present no difficulty.

Οἱ Ἀλεξανδρινοί ἔνιωθαν βέβαια
πού ἦσαν λόγια αὐτά καί θεατρικά.
Ἀλλά ἡ ἡμέρα ἤτανε ζεστή καί ποιητική,
ὁ οὐρανός ἕνα γαλάζιο ἀνοιχτό,
τό Ἀλεξανδρινό Γυμνάσιον ἕνα
θριαμβικό κατόρθωμα τῆς τέχνης,
τῶν αὐλικῶν ἡ πολυτέλεια ἔκτακτη,
ὁ Καισαρίων ὅλο χάρις κι' ἐμορφιά
(τῆς Κλεοπάτρας υἱός, αἷμα τῶν Λαγιδῶν)
κι' οἱ Ἀλεξανδρινοί ἔτρεχαν πιά στήν ἑορτή
κι' ἐνθουσιάζονταν κι' ἐπευφημοῦσαν
ἑλληνικά κι' αἰγυπτιακά καί ποιοί ἑβραΐκα,
γοητευμένοι, μέ τ' ὡραῖο θέαμα,
μ' ὅλο πού, βέβαια, ἤξεραν τί ἄξιζαν αὐτά,
τί κούφια λόγια ἦσανε αὐτές οἱ βασιλεῖες.

Κ. ΚΑΒΑΦΗΣ

KEY TO THE EXERCISES

EXERCISE 1

1. Mother is good.
2. The car is very big.
3. The night is wonderful.
4. The large bar is full.
5. Father is very good.
6. She is a beautiful girl.
7. She is a very good mother.
8. He is a very good man (person).
9. Life is difficult.
10. Breakfast is ready.

EXERCISE 2

1. *-ό.* 2. *-ή.* 3. *-ο.* 4. *-ός.* 5. *-ή.* 6. *εἶναι.* 7. *-ος.* 8. *-η.* 9. *-ο.* 10. *-α.* 11. *-ο.*

EXERCISE 3

1. That woman was very beautiful.
2. This child is very happy.
3. The night-club was not full.
4. George is very silly.
5. Life is beautiful.
6. Mother is a very good woman.
7. Father is a wonderful man.
8. Mary was very serious.
9. This garden isn't big.
10. This isn't correct.

11. Russell is a great philosopher.
12. Plato was a great philosopher.

EXERCISE 4

1. The nights are cool.
2. The days are not very cool.
3. The consequences were serious.
4. Money is indispensable.
5. These young men are happy.
6. Two green eyes.
7. Lies are bad.
8. Black eyes are beautiful.
9. Athens is enchanting.
10. One child was here. The other children were very far away.
11. These two rooms are large and cool.
12. The men, women and children are happy.
13. A lot of money is not necessary.
14. Fair hair is beautiful.
15. The other woman was not very old.
16. This colour is green.
17. This water is cold.

EXERCISE 5

1. *-α.* 2. *-οι.* 3. *-ός.* 4. *-ο.* 5. *-α.* 6. *-ες.* 7. *-α.* 8. *-ή.* 9. *-η.* 10. *-α.*

EXERCISE 6

1. Your sister is sad.
2. Our uncle is very good, but he's poor.
3. Their hands are black.

4. My aunt was very happy.
5. His head is a bit small.
6. Her hair is fair and her eyes blue.
7. His new car is black.
8. My house is small but cool.
9. My brother is thin but very strong.
10. George is a friend of mine but John isn't.
11. His family are poor.
12. Her hands are thin.

EXERCISE 7

1. This room is his.
2. These are our own children.
3. Is this hat yours?
4. The middle of the day was very hot.
5. These cigarettes are hers.
6. His voice is very powerful (loud).
7. George is one of us (*or* one of our men).
8. His feet are big.
9. This is my own affair.
10. It is not your business (*or* your sort of work).
11. Are all these cigarettes yours?
12. His heart is a very warm one.

EXERCISE 8

1. My sister's house is very large.
2. The garden of our house is small but beautiful.
3. This Englishman's name is John.
4. This English lady's name is Margaret.
5. Mrs. Benaki's party was wonderful.
6. The midday sun is very hot.
7. Andrew's hair is black.

8. Mr. Andoni's family are very rich.
9. The light in your little room isn't very strong.
10. Spring in Athens is enchanting.
11. The Aegean sun is hot and pleasant.
12. This woman's eyes are very black.
13. My friend's office is a bit small, but cool and pleasant.
14. The engine of your car is very powerful.
15. That young Englishwoman's hair is fair.

EXERCISE 9

1. The rooms of large houses are cool.
2. The life of workmen is hard.
3. My brother is only eight years old.
4. The engines of good cars are powerful.
5. My young sister is four years old.
6. Beautiful women's hands are slender.
7. The story of the three children and their poor mother was very moving.

EXERCISE 10

1. I want a little water.
2. He* is in Cyprus.
3. The motor-car is in the garage.
4. The whole family are at home.
5. I have no money.
6. I have joy in my heart.
7. The man in the tall hat is on the veranda.
8. That woman with the grey hair is my mother.
9. My brother went to England and my sister to Greece.
10. My room is above yours.
11. He was in his office for a long time.

* εἶναι may be rendered by *he is* or *she is* or *it is* or *they are*, according to the context.

12. Our house is near the sea.
13. His feet are in the water.
14. I want a glass of wine.
15. My uncle has come from America.
16. I saw your friend John in Athens.
17. This hat is for Costa.
18. Give me a glass of water.
19. Give me three bottles of wine.
20. My father has gone to Athens to get work.

EXERCISE 11

1. I saw your brother in the street.
2. The water is on the table.
3. My sister is in France.
4. My father's car is near the entrance to the cinema.
5. My uncle's got a lot of money.
6. My young brother is only five years old.
7. That man with the grey hair is my father.
8. Where's Andrew? He's at the cinema.
9. Where's your brother? He's gone to the sea with his friends.
10. The light in this room isn't strong.
11. Where's Costas now? He's at his office.
12. Where's my overcoat? It's in the living room.
13. Give me a little wine, please.
14. Now I have no money.

EXERCISE 12

1. *Ὁ πατέρας μου εἶναι στό Λονδῖνο.*
2. *Τά παιδιά εἶναι κοντά στή θάλασσα.*
3. *Τό κρασί εἶναι μέσα στό μπουκάλι.*
4. *Τό μπουκάλι εἶναι πάνω στό τραπέζι.*
5. *Ἔχω ἕναν ἀδελφό καί μιάν ἀδελφή.*

6. Ὁ Γιῶργος πῆγε στή Θεσσαλονίκη.
7. Ὁ φίλος σου εἶναι στή βεράντα.
8. Τό τηλέφωνο εἶναι στό σαλόνι.
9. Ποῦ εἶναι τό πρωϊνό μου;
10. Τό πρωϊνό εἶναι στήν κουζίνα.
11. Ποῦ εἶναι τά παιδιά;
12. Τά παιδιά εἶναι στόν κῆπο.
13. Ἐκεῖνος ὁ ψηλός ἄνθρωπος εἶναι ὁ θεῖος μου.
14. Πῆγε στήν Ἀγγλία μέ ἀεροπλάνο.
15. Πῆγε μέ τόν ἀδελφό μου.
16. Ἡ μητέρα μου δέν εἶναι στό σπίτι τώρα.
17. Ὅλη ἡ οἰκογένεια πῆγε στή θάλασσα.
18. Δέν ἔχω πολλά λεφτά.
19. Θέλω λίγο νερό.
20. Ὁ ἀδελφός μου εἶναι στη δουλειά του, τώρα.
21. Τό τηλέφωνο δέν εἶναι κοντά στήν πόρτα.
22. Τό παιδί εἶναι κάτω ἀπό τό τραπέζι.
23. Αὐτό τό κρασί εἶναι γιά τόν πατέρα σου.
24. Δόσε μου λίγο νερό, παρακαλῶ.
25. Δόσε μου δέκα τσιγάρα καί ἕνα κουτί σπίρτα.

EXERCISE 13

1. τρεῖς καί δεκαπέντε. 2. δώδεκα. 3. ἐννιά παρά δέκα. 4. ἑφτά παρά τέταρτο. 5. τέσσερεις καί πέντε. 6. ἐννέα καί δέκα. 7. ἑφτάμιση. 8. δεκάμιση. 9. μία. 10. τέσσερεις παρά τέταρτο. 11. μία καί τέσσερα. 12. ὀγδόντα . . . εἴκοσι. 13. ἐνενήντα . . . τριάντα. 14. ἑξηνταπέντε . . . πέντε.

EXERCISE 14

1. Saturday is the last day of the week.
2. Costas went to the sea on Wednesday.

3. Sunday is a pleasant day.
4. A week has seven days.
5. Renos is (the) second (pupil) in his class.
6. Five hundredths are equal to one twentieth.
7. One thirteenth is equal to two twenty-sixths.
8. Half an hour is equal to thirty minutes.

EXERCISE 15

1. Your house is smaller than ours.
2. John is bigger (older) than Peter.
3. This is the best of all.
4. Plato was the greatest philosopher of (in) Greece.
5. This work is most difficult.
6. This wine is stronger than that.
7. Myconos is more beautiful but much hotter than Kavalla.
8. England is bigger than Ireland.

EXERCISE 16

1. *γυρίσω*. 2. *προσέξω*. 3. *σταματήσω*. 4. *ανάψω*. 5. *θαρρήσω*. 6. *μπορέσω*. 7. *μοιάσω*. 8. *παρακολουθήσω*. 9. *ζητήσω*. 10. *πιάσω*. 11. *κρύψω*. 12. *χαμογελάσω*. 13. *φτάσω*. 14. *προχωρήσω*. 15. *ξυπνήσω*. 16. *κόψω*. 17. *γεμίσω*. 18. *προσπαθήσω*. 19. *ξέρω*. 20. *ζήσω*. 21. *ρωτήσω*. 22. *έχω*. 23. *νομίσω*. 24. *μιλήσω*. 25. *δουλέψω*. 26. *δείξω*. 27. *προτείνω*. 28. *φύγω*. 29. *πιώ*. 30. *καταλάβω*. 31. *πω*. 32. *περάσω*. 33. *δω*. 34. *δόσω*. 35. *μείνω*.

EXERCISE 17

1. *δείχνω*. 2. *φέρω*. 3. *κρύβω*. 4. *συνεχίζω*. 5. *χορεύω*. 6. *απαντώ*. 7. *τρώγω*. 8. *λέγω*.

9. κουνῶ. 10. γελῶ. 11. ζητῶ. 12. φροντίζω. 13. προχωρῶ. 14. κοιτάζω. 15. μπορῶ. 16. ἔχω. 17. φτάνω. 18. κάνω. 19. ἐξετάζω. 20. κλείω. 21. κρατῶ. 22. χαλῶ. 23. προσπαθῶ. 24. βάζω. 25. καταλαβαίνω. 26. βλέπω.

EXERCISE 18

1. I go to work by car.
2. I have only three pounds.
3. I take (attend) piano lessons.
4. I see an aeroplane.
5. I want a little water.
6. I have one brother and two sisters.
7. I know your uncle.
8. Now I am eating.

EXERCISE 19

1. I shall speak with courage.
2. I shall go to America.
3. On Saturday I shall go to the sea.
4. I shall eat roast lamb.
5. I shall go to the cinema and see *Alice in Wonderland.*
6. I shall travel all through the East.
7. I will answer your question.
8. Tomorrow I shall wake up at seven in the morning.
9. Tomorrow I shall be reading from 3 until 6 in the afternoon.

EXERCISE 20

1. In the autumn I shall take (attend) English lessons.
2. Do you see that aeroplane on the horizon?

3. We have money but we don't have quietness.
4. Would you like (do you want) a little water?
5. Father is going (will go) to Germany.
6. Where are you staying?
7. I am staying at the Hotel Astoria.
8. Do you know my uncle? Yes, but he isn't a friend of mine.
9. I don't understand.
10. What do you want, please?
11. Nothing, thank you.
12. He smokes ten cigarettes a day.
13. Why are you laughing, may I ask?

EXERCISE 21

1. *Κλείω τό παράθυρο.*
2. *Θά πᾶμε στή Γαλλία.*
3. *Δέ θέλουν τσάϊ.*
4. *Δουλεύω στήν πόλη.*
5. *Ἔχεις πολλά χρήματα;*
6. *Παρακολουθῶ μαθήματα μουσικῆς.*
7. *Βλέπεις μιά βάρκα στή θάλασσα;*
8. *Ὁ πατέρας μου δέ βλέπει πολύ μα κριά.*
9. *Θά πᾶμε στήν Ἀμερική καί ὁ Γιάννης θά πάει στή Γαλλία.*
10. *Καπνίζετε;*
11. *Δέν καπνίζω.*
12. *Δέν πίνουμε μπύρα.*
13. *Θέλω ἕνα ποτήρι κρασί.*
14. *Θέλουμε ἕνα σπίτι κοντά στή θάλασσα.*
15. *Αὔριο θά πᾶμε στή Μύκονο.*
16. *Δέ θέλω τσάϊ, θέλω καφέ.*

EXERCISE 22

1. γύρισα. 2. νόμισα. 3. μάζεψα. 4. ἔκοψα. 5. ἔφερα. 6. ἔφτασα. 7. ἔψαξα. 8. εἶδα. 9. κατέβηκα. 10. ἀπάντησα. 11. πῆγα. 12. κράτησα. 13. ρώτησα. 14. μπόρεσα. 15. κούνησα. 16. σταμάτησα. 17. ἔζησα. 18. προχώρησα. 19. ἔφαγα. 20. ἔμεινα. 21. ἔχασα. 22. εἶχα.

EXERCISE 23

1. The officers left the meeting.
2. The blood went (up) to his head.
3. This man knew a lot.
4. The fat man didn't answer.
5. I sent my mother a packet.
6. They lived for three years in Naples.
7. My father always had money.
8. Yesterday I saw George on the train.
9. Mrs. Lambridi nodded her head.
10. At the door Helena turned round.
11. I stayed at the hotel.
12. He went close to him and spoke to him.
13. They continued their conversation upon various questions.
14. I received your letter.
15. Light (*or* he lit) a match.
16. Come home (*or* he came home) early.

EXERCISE 24

1. *Πῆγε στήν 'Ιταλία.*
2. *Πήγαμε στή Γερμανία.*
3. *Πῆγαν στήν 'Αγγλία.*

4. *Πήγατε στή Γαλλία.*
5. *Πῆγες στήν 'Αμερική;*
6. *Πήγατε στό θέατρο χθές;*
7. *"Ακουσες;*
8. *'Ο Πέτρος δέν κατάλαβε.*
9. *"Εμειναν στό σπίτι μας γιά πολύν καιρό.*
10. *Εἶδα τόν ἀδελφό σου στή Λευκοσία.*
11. *Διάβασα τήν "Αννα Καρενίνα.*
12. *Σταμάτησε γιά λίγο, χαμογέλασε καί ὕστερα εἶπε . . .*
13. *"Εκλεισε τά μάτια της.*
14. *Χτές ξύπνησα πολύ νωρίς.*
15. *"Εβαλαν τό αὐτοκίνητο στό γκαράζ.*
16. *"Εφυγε χθές τό πρωΐ.*

EXERCISE 25

1. From a place of entertainment there came (the sound of) dance music.
2. Lilika didn't understand.
3. *She* was looking him in the eyes.
4. As I was going to work I saw George.
5. He was singing the whole afternoon.
6. As I was running I fell down.
7. The fat man remained quiet.
8. He was talking to the girl with grey eyes.
9. The others were not talking.
10. His brain was working coolly.
11. They were not staying with them.
12. He was trying to find the child's mental level.
13. While he was going up the stairs he heard loud voices.
14. Charalambos was drinking by himself at the bar.
15. At that moment Alkis was lighting his cigarette.
16. For days the engine of his car had not been going well.
17. He found the young man fatuous.

EXERCISE 26

1. Can I go tomorrow?
2. He wanted to speak but couldn't.
3. Now you must go.
4. I can't (don't know how to) speak well, but this I want to say: we all love our work.
5. You can take a taxi.
6. Zeno began to run.
7. It isn't worth your going to Athens without seeing the Acropolis.
8. He couldn't sleep a wink.
9. What do you want to say? (what do you mean?).
10. I don't want to say anything (I don't mean anything).
11. He didn't want to lose his happiness.
12. You must leave at once.

EXERCISE 27

1. *Δέ θέλω νά πάω στό σχολεῖο.*
2. *Μπορῶ νά ἔχω ἕνα φλυντζάνι τσάϊ, παρακαλῶ;*
3. *Μπορεῖτε νά μοῦ δόσετε ἕνα ποτήρι νερό;*
4. *Δέν ἤθελε νά πάει μαζί σας στό σινεμά.*
5. *Πρέπει νά διαβάσω αὐτό τό βιβλίο ἀπόψε.*
6. *Ἄρχισε νά γελᾶ.*
7. *Θέλω νά φάω σταφύλια.*
8. *Δέν ἤθελαν νά χάσουν τά λεφτά τους.*

EXERCISE 28

1. I have lost all my money.
2. Surprise had completely extinguished his anger.
3. He lost time but he had gained a good friend.
4. I haven't seen this work of art.
5. He had lit his cigarette and was waiting.

6. They had not heard the news.
7. You hadn't closed the door.
8. I have never been there in my life.

EXERCISE 29

1. Shut your (sing.) eyes.
2. Shut your (pl.) eyes.
3. Stop joking.
4. Look what I've brought.
5. Go to your work.
6. Come and see with your (own) eyes.
7. Wake up, for it's 10 o'clock.
8. Write your name.
9. Stop here.
10. Begin to sing.
11. Write these letters.
12. Go to your uncle.
13. Stay here.
14. Don't turn off the light.
15. Don't say anything.
16. Don't go away.
17. Don't go now.
18. Speak slowly, please.
19. Go upstairs.
20. Get down.

EXERCISE 30

1. *Μή τρέχεις.*
2. *Τρέξε γρήγορα.*
3. *Πήγαινε σιγά.*
4. *Ἄκουε τόν πατέρα σου.*
5. *Κλεῖσε τ'αὐτιά σου.*

6. *Ἄνοιξε τήν πόρτα.*
7. *Μή γελᾶτε.*
8. *Μή φάγεις.*
9. *Πήγαινε στό σπίτι σου.*
10. *Γράφε.*
11. *Μή γράφεις.*
12. *Δέν πρέπει νά πιεῖς πολύ κρασί* or *Νά μή πιεῖς πολύ κρασί.*
13. *Μή μιλᾶς.*
14. *Μή κουνᾶς τά χέρια σου.*
15. *Μεῖνε ἐδῶ γιά μισή ὥρα.*
16. *Ρίξε τή μπάλα.*
17. *Συνέχισε τήν ἱστορία.*
18. *Μή μέ ἀφίσεις μόνο.*

EXERCISE 31

1. He had a lot of money but he spent it.
2. I know you very well.
3. They call me Lilian.
4. He took him by the hand and spoke to him.
5. She was asking him about the quality.
6. My father sent me to a private school.
7. He wasn't expecting it.
8. He looked him in the eyes.
9. He put him in his place.
10. I bought a book and read it in one day.
11. He didn't believe it.
12. I have been following (*or* observing) you for a long time.
13. I thought you were a Russian.
14. He squeezed his hand.
15. She stayed beside him.
16. I've never seen it in my life.
17. He hadn't understood her.

18. He was trying (*lit.* searching) to find it.
19. Let me alone.
20. Tomorrow wake me early.
21. Let me go away.
22. He saw him and shouted to him.
23. Tell me the truth.
24. Don't say those things to me.
25. Can you see her?
26. Why do you tell me these things?
27. Would you like me to show you the garden?
28. They are staying with us.
29. I have known you for some time.
30. You won't do it.
31. Go, they are waiting for you.
32. They were running round him.
33. I have a good bit more to tell you.
34. I can't do it.
35. Why did you let him go away?
36. Ring me up tomorrow morning.
37. Give me three stamps.
38. I'll tell it to you.

EXERCISE 32

1. *Γύρισε καί τόν κοίταξε.*
2. *Δέ μοῦ εἶπε τίποτε.*
3. *Πήγαινε μόνος σου.*
4. *Ἔλα δίπλα μου.*
5. *Φέρε μου ἕνα κομμάτι χαρτί.*
6. *Μέ φωνάζουν.*
7. *Τί σοῦ εἶπε ὁ πατέρας;*
8. *Τόν ρώτησαν πολλές ἐρωτήσεις.*
9. *Τηλεφώνα μου ἀπόψε.*
10. *Δεῖξε μου τόν κῆπο.*

11. *Πρέπει πάντα νά λές τήν ἀλήθεια.*
12. *Δέ σέ πιστεύω.*
13. *Δόσε μου δυό μπουκάλια μπύρα.*
14. *Δέν τόν ξέρω.*
15. *Δέν τόν εἶδαν.*
16. *Ὅλη ἡ οἰκογένεια σέ περιμένει.*
17. *Πάρε μου ἕνα ταξί.*
18. *Μίλα μου γι' αὐτή τήν ὑπόθεση.*
19. *Πῆγε κοντά τους.*
20. *Καλημέρα σας.*

EXERCISE 33

1. I am ashamed of her.
2. Do you remember me?
3. You seem proud of it.
4. Now we are on the sixth floor.
5. He is at the office.
6. I am sorry for you.
7. He got up suddenly.
8. The girl was surprised.
9. Alec has married Vera.
10. For the first time Philip felt afraid.
11. He stood opposite him.
12. The famous party was given.
13. He found himself alone.
14. She seemed moved.
15. She was standing beside him.
16. On a lighted veranda could be seen two couples dancing.
17. He was getting ready to leave.
18. He hadn't understood her.
19. He wants to marry her.
20. I couldn't go to sleep all night long.
21. Go to sleep.

22. Think carefully.
23. Don't get ready.
24. Stop here.

EXERCISE 34

1. *Δέ σέ θυμᾶμαι.*
2. *Δέ μπορῶ νά σκεφθῶ τώρα.*
3. *Φοβήθηκα πολύ.*
4. *Δέ σέ λυπᾶμαι.*
5. *Ἑτοιμάστηκε πολύ γρήγορα.*
6. *Στάθηκε κοντά μου.*
7. *Δέ μπορῶ νά κοιμηθῶ αὐτές τίς μέρες.*
8. *Μή χαθεῖς.*
9. *Ποῦ βρίσκεται τώρα;*
10. *Κοιμήσου.*

EXERCISE 35

1. You are a person without will-power.
2. We are very tired.
3. They sat down round a small low table.
4. I shall come tomorrow.
5. She was sitting beside him.
6. He told him to sit down.
7. I was then nine years old.
8. He didn't know what was happening.
9. Don't sit there.
10. Let's go to the theatre.
11. Your talk was wonderful.
12. I am going to be an engineer.
13. It's mine.
14. What do you want, please?

EXERCISE 36

1. Whom do you want?
2. What do *you* think?
3. Whose is this hat?
4. I hate myself.
5. I'll give 3 drachmas to you and 3 to your brother.
6. We are not millionaires.
7. Who did I give my watch to?
8. Don't ask *us*.
9. It was I who said it.
10. I know myself.
11. Whose is this box of matches?

EXERCISE 37

1. He always had money.
2. Go over opposite and ask.
3. He put down his glass quietly on the mantelpiece.
4. I can see clearly with these spectacles.
5. He was scrutinizing him piercingly.
6. He is already fifteen years old.
7. What do you want us to do? he said suddenly.
8. He had completely forgotten her.
9. Make haste.
10. We went together but he came back.
11. Go straight on and then to the right.
12. George goes to bed late, and wakes up early in the morning.
13. He waved his hand to me, like that.

EXERCISE 38

1. *Ἔλα ἐδῶ γρήγορα.*
2. *Ἔλα πίσω τώρα.*

3. Ἔφαγε καί ἤπιε ἀρκετά.
4. Καλύτερα νά ἔρθεις αὔριο.
5. Δέν ἔχει ἔρθει.
6. Περπάτα πολύ σιγά.
7. Ἔλα πάλι.
8. Τώρα γελᾶς ἀλλά ὕστερα θά κλάψεις.
9. Αὔριο θά εἶναι καλύτερα.
10. Τήν κοίταζε περίεργα.

EXERCISE 39

1. He went there usually in the afternoons.
2. New York is very far from here.
3. I am speaking to you sincerely.
4. Unfortunately I have no money with me.
5. I will come at three exactly.
6. You didn't write to us: consequently we didn't come.
7. Haris is very consistent and sincere, but he is not punctual.
8. Shakespeare is a profound writer.
9. This river is very deep.
10. Go away. Otherwise we shall send you away.
11. He spoke continuously, but I couldn't understand what he was saying.
12. I simply want you to leave me in peace.
13. I don't usually go to the cinema, but yesterday I went as an exception.

EXERCISE 40

1. He got up suddenly, pushing away the chair behind him.
2. Thank you, he said, smiling.
3. He was going (along) singing.
4. Others get merry drinking.

5. He kept talking without sense, changing the subject.
6. No, replied he, avoiding her gaze.
7. He had approached noiselessly, and was watching them, smiling.
8. He repeated the sentence, emphasizing every word.
9. He was walking along looking behind him.
10. She spoke continuously, moving her hand.

EXERCISE 41

1. *Θά πάω τρέχοντας.*
2. *Ἦρθε τραγουδώντας μέ δυνατή φωνή.*
3. *Ἔφτασε μή μπορώντας νά πεῖ λέξη.*
4. *Ξάπλωσε κάτω κοιτάζοντας τό ταβάνι.*
5. *Κάθισαν γιά λίγο μιλώντας στό διευθυντή.*
6. *Ἔφυγαν πηγαίνοντας ἀνατολικά.*

EXERCISE 42

1. He was drunk and didn't know what he was saying.
2. Today I (*fem.*) am very glad.
3. Helen seemed moved.
4. He was dressed with much elegance.
5. She had her eyes continuously fixed upon him.
6. Mrs. Brown nodded her head with a happy smile.
7. Three men were sitting on a lighted veranda and talking.
8. All these things are whims of a spoilt child.

EXERCISE 43

1. *Γιατί εἶσαι τόσο λυπημένος;*
2. *Ἦταν τρομαγμένος.*
3. *Εἴμαστε προσκαλεσμένοι στό πάρτυ τῆς κυρίας Πετρίδη.*

4. *Δούλεψα πολύ καί εἶμαι κουρασμένος.*
5. *Δέν ξέρω τό λόγο ἀλλά εἶμαι πολύ δυστυχισμένος.*
6. *Ὁ Μίλτων ἔγραψε τό " Χαμένο Παράδεισο".*
7. *Ἦταν βυθισμένος στίς σκέψεις του.*
8. *Εἶμαι θυμωμένος μαζί σου.*

EXERCISE 44

1. This seat is very far forward.
2. It is almost impossible for me to believe it.
3. His father has a fairly large (amount of) property.
4. I want a coffee, rather sweet.
5. Is it so difficult for you to do me this favour?
6. Your son's awfully intelligent.
7. This person is completely unknown to me.
8. It's very funny.
9. You are very polite.
10. This wine is even better.
11. Do you want some water? Yes, but not much.
12. This food is better than that.
13. I can't see very far.
14. I woke up very late and went to work at ten o'clock.

EXERCISE 45

1. Where do you want to go? he said to him suddenly.
2. Who will prevent me?
3. How old are you?
4. Have you come to me drunk, may I ask?
5. Which is your family?
6. What are you thinking of doing?
7. Why do you ask?
8. How is your father? Very well, thank you.
9. I wonder if he will remember me.

10. How are you? Not so bad.
11. Whose is this bicycle?

EXERCISE 46

1. *Γιατί φεύγεις τόσο νωρίς;*
2. *Τί θέλεις νά πεῖς;*
3. *Γιατί ὄχι;*
4. *Μήπως μοῦ κρύβεις τίποτε;*
5. *Τί μποροῦσε νά κάνει μόνος του;*
6. *Τί ὥρα εἶναι, παρακαλῶ;*
7. *Ὥστε φεύγεις;*
8. *Μήπως νομίζεις πώς μπορῶ νά σέ περιμένω δυό ὧρες;*
9. *Γιατί μοῦ τά λές αὐτά;*

EXERCISE 47

1. We left when the play ended.
2. He kept talking because he wanted to forget.
3. He angered him because he spoke to him sharply.
4. Now he was seeing that artists had a special value in life.
5. They went out of the room after they had turned off the light.
6. He was laughing, while secretly (within him) he was very upset.
7. Tomorrow when you are well, you thank me.
8. Don't think I'm ashamed of this.
9. He said he would come at eight.
10. The officer wasn't there but he knew all the details.
11. Don't you think we have delayed enough?
12. I've had my adventures. I think you must have heard about them.
13. I am waiting in case he comes.

14. I remained there until the train started.
15. They were happy to see him again in good health.

EXERCISE 48

1. *Πρόσεξε ὅτι τά φῶτα ἦταν σβυσμένα μέσα στό σπίτι.*
2. *Γιά μιά στιγμή φάνηκε σά νά ἤθελε νά πεῖ κάτι ἀλλά μετάνιωσε.*
3. *Τόν ἄφισε ἀφοῦ γύρισε καί τόν κοίταξε θυμωμένα.*
4. *Δέ μπορῶ νά μιλῶ καλά ἀλλά θέλω νά πῶ αὐτό.*
5. *Φεύγει ὅποτε ἔρχεσαι ἐσύ.*
6. *Συνήθιζε νά μᾶς λέει νά μή καπνίζουμε ἀλλά ἐκεῖνος κάπνιζε πολύ.*
7. *Ἔμεινα ἐκεῖ ὡσότου ἦρθανε.*
8. *Καθώς περπατοῦσα στό δρόμο εἶδα κάτι ἀσυνήθιστο.*
9. *Φοβόταν μήπως τόν ἄφινε ὁ πατέρας του.*
10. *Κάνε ὅπως θέλεις.*
11. *Ἔλα, ἄνκαι δέν εἶναι πολύ ἀνάγκη.*
12. *Πήγαινε ὅπου θέλεις.*
13. *Ἦρθε μόλις τό ἄκουσε.*

EXERCISE

1. It's the Englishman who was here at the time of the occupation.
2. He came to Greece with a good bit of money that he had made in America.
3. At this moment when we are speaking, you owe your rent.
4. It was something he wasn't expecting.
5. If he stayed silent it wasn't because he had nothing to say.
6. Opposite were seen two couples dancing.

7. I saw Vassos who was enjoying the morning on the veranda.
8. He didn't want to be deprived of the wealth which had so unexpectedly come (*lit.* fallen) to him.
9. Do what you like.
10. He went to find him at John's place, which he usually frequented in the mornings.
11. I am a person who wants to give you back the happiness you have lost, the wealth that belongs to you, your family that you have not had joy in.

EXERCISE 50

1. *Ἂν θέλεις νά ἔρθεις, ἔλα ἀπόψε.*
2. *Αὐτό εἶναι τό βιβλίο πού σοῦ ἔδοσα.*
3. *Τή στιγμή πού κάθισαν ἡ μουσική ἄρχισε νά παίζει.*
4. *Εἶναι ὁ ἄνθρωπος πού μᾶς βοήθησε σέ μιά δύσκολη στιγμή.*
5. *Πῆγε στό καφενεῖο ὅπου συνήθιζαν νά πηγαίνουν οἱ φίλοι του.*
6. *Εἴδαμε δυό γυναῖκες πού συζητοῦσαν.*

EXERCISE 51

1. I don't want either to see you or you to see me.
2. Either you go or your brother.
3. I am forced to stay at home, not only because I want to work but also because I am waiting for an important phone call.
4. In any case they will have started off at three.
5. We should have started off at three if you had come in time.
6. I should very much like to see *King Lear* tonight.
7. Shall I stay or go?

8. You ought to have written to me as soon as you got my letter.
9. You ought to have come at once.
10. He spoke to me very politely as if he didn't know me.
11. Let us sing all together.
12. He used to drink in order to forget his troubles.
13. May you win.
14. I don't like getting up very early.

EXERCISE 52

1. The time has come for the big decision.
2. My wife takes care of all household matters (*lit.* things of the house).
3. Napkin in hand he went to the window.
4. He took the photograph from Costa's hands, looked at it with care, and gave it back to him laughing.
5. He stretched himself out in the armchair where a short time before the unknown gentleman was sitting.
6. From the sea a cold wind was blowing.
7. I shall be in the library from ten in the morning till five in the afternoon.
8. Come and call for me after five.
9. He squeezed the brief-case under his arm.
10. Outside the door a taxi was waiting.
11. She looked after me like a mother.
12. I said a kind word (*lit.* good words) for you to him.
13. This man strikingly resembles my father.
14. I saw him after three years.

EXERCISE 53

1. *Δέ θά μποροῦσα νά κάνω τίποτε χωρίς τή βοήθειά σου.*
2. *Ἔφτασε στό σπίτι του πολύ ἀργά.*

3. *Μοιάζει σάν ἕνα ἀστέρι τοῦ σιά.*
4. *Προχώρησε πρός τό μέσο τοῦ δματίου.*
5. *Τό σπίτι μου εἶναι κοντά στό κέντρο τῆς πόλης.*
6. *Κατοικῶ σ'ἕνα διαμέρισμα μαζί μέ δυό φίλους μου.*
7. *Ἡ πέννα σου εἶναι πάνω στό ραδιόφωνο.*
8. *Τά μῆλα εἶναι μέσα στό καλάθι.*
9. *Ἀπό τίς πέντε ὥς τίς ἑφτά θά εἶμαι στό σπίτι.*
10. *Τό βλέμμα της ἔλεγε πολύ περισσότερα ἀπό τά λόγια της.*
11. *Τό αὐτοκίνητο σταμάτησε πλάϊ στό πεζοδρόμιο.*
12. *Κάθισαν ὅλοι γύρω στή φωτιά.*
13. *Ξεκίνησαν γιά τόν Πειραιά..*
14. *Πῆγε στήν Ἀγγλία μέ ἀεροπλάνο.*
15. *Θά πάω στή Γερμανία ἀεροπορικῶς ἤ σιδηροδρομικῶς.*

EXERCISE 54

1. Everybody is restless.
2. Some days are very hot and some are very cold.
3. Three hundred Spartans under Leonidas fought at Thermopylae.
4. Some gentleman came and was looking for you.
5. Most people are neither stupid nor clever.
6. He lost a thousand pounds at cards.
7. Everything at its (proper) time.
8. Many workers are without work.
9. He told me something very improbable.
10. I spent 438 pounds 12 shillings and 8 pence.
11. The last war started in 1939 and ended in 1945.

EXERCISE 55

(*a*) *χίλια ἑφτακόσια σαράντα τρία.*
(*b*) *ἑξακόσια τριάντα τέσσερα.*

(*c*) *σαρανταδύο χιλιάδες ἑφτακόσια ἑβδομήντα.*
(*d*) *δέκα χιλιάδες πεντακόσια.*
(*e*) *ὀκτακόσιες τριάντα ἕξι χιλιάδες ἑκατόν εἰκοσιτέσσερα.*
(*f*) *τετρακόσια ἕξι.*
(*g*) *εἰκοσιτρεῖς χιλιάδες διακόσια πέντε.*
(*h*) *ἕνα ἑκατομμύριο τριακόσιες ἑβδομήντα ἕξι χιλιάδες διακόσια εἴκοσι ὀκτώ.*

EXERCISE 56

Good morning.—How are you?—Very well, thanks. And you?—Yes thank you (*lit.* the same).—How's the work going? Same as usual (*lit.* quietness).—It's a pity one has to work in such wonderful weather.—I absolutely agree. —But next week we have two days off.—How's your brother? He's all right. He was asking me about you the other day.—Please give him my best regards. Goodbye.

EXERCISE 57

Next week I intend to go on a trip to Mykonos for a few days. Would you like to come with me?—I should like to very much, but I don't know if I shall be able to manage it. But I shall try, and I'll let you know tomorrow. I am very fond of the Aegean islands, and specially Mykonos.— Try and arrange to come, and we'll have a wonderful time. —I can't promise you, but I think it's almost certain that I shall come.

EXERCISE 58

Where shall we go tonight? Shall we go to the cinema, the theatre or some dance?—I think there's a good film at the

Palace. Laurence Olivier and Jean Simmons are in it.—Is it Shakespeare's *Hamlet*?—Yes, that's it.—Do you think we shall find seats easily?—Let's try, and if we don't find seats let's go to some dance. Or would you like to go and eat and drink in the Plaka?—Just as you think. I leave it to you. But ring me up at five this afternoon (and tell me) what you've decided.

EXERCISE 59

I want to go to Achilles Street, but I've forgotten the way. Please can you show me the way?—Go straight ahead, and at the third turning go left. After that take the second turning right, and you'll find yourself in Achilles Street.—Thank you very much.—If you have any difficulty, ask the policeman standing at the corner of the road.—All right. But I expect I shall find it without any difficulty.

EXERCISE 60

Can I speak to Mr. Aleko, please?—One minute, please.—Hallo?—Mr. Aleko?—Speaking.—Mr. Panos here. It's about the question of a flat which I mentioned to you the other day. Have you got one available now?—One moment and I'll have a look, Mr. Panos . . . Hallo? You're very lucky, Mr. Panos. I have just the one to suit you admirably. When can you see it?—I can see it today or tomorrow, but after six.—All right. I'll give you the address and you can go there on your own.—Thank you very much. I'm much obliged to you.—*I'm* obliged to *you*.

EXERCISE 61

Can you please tell me where I can change some English pounds?—Certainly. You should go to some tourist agency or a bank.—Up to what time are the banks open in summer?—Till three in the afternoon. Look, down there is the Bank of Greece. There you can change all foreign currencies.—Do you know what the rate for the pound is these days?—The gold sovereign is about three hundred drachmas, and the paper pound about eighty-four.—Thank you very much for the information. Good-bye.

EXERCISE 62

Where is there a good restaurant?—In University Street.—It is dear?—Medium.—Can I have a menu, please?—Here you are, sir.—I've got some wonderful roast lamb.—Good. Bring us two portions, with salad. And some cold water.—Would you like some wine?—Yes, a bottle of retsina . . . Well, when shall we go and see the Acropolis?—Let's go this afternoon, if you like.—All right, what time?—Half past three.—Where shall we meet?—At Omonia (Concord Square), outside the Avra Hotel.—Are you staying near there?—No, I'm staying with friends at Kypseli, but it's only a few minutes by trolley-bus. Are you near Omonia?—Yes, I'm at a little hotel called the "Cleanliness".—What does it cost you?—I pay 40 drachmas for a single room with breakfast.—Are you satisfied?—On the whole. Besides, it's quite convenient for me as it's in the centre of the city.—Waiter, how much do we owe?—(Coming) at once. I will bring you the bill. 64 drachmas. Here is your change.—Thank you very much.—Did you like the meal?—Yes, it was excellent.

EXERCISE 63

On the fifteenth of August, which is (the Assumption) of Our Lady, everybody goes for an excursion, either to the sea or the mountains. On that day they wake up very early, prepare food and drinks and put them in big baskets, with glasses, plates and knives and forks. Some go in private cars, others in buses. Since there are a lot of people, there is a great crush everywhere to find seats. Many will not go sitting but standing. But it doesn't matter, as the journey is not long.

The sea is not far away, and all those who are going to it will come across a beautiful beach. Their first task is to look round for a shady place. Of course everyone prefers a big thick pine-tree near the shore. The young ones immediately put on their bathing costumes and rush into the water. The Greek sea is enchanting, blue as the Greek sky, and as clean and clear as crystal. They swim, play games in the water and sunbathe for hours on end.

At midday some people eat in taverns. But the majority spread (a picnic) on the ground and eat the food they have brought with them. There is no lack of wine or iced beer. And the fruit in season, too, is indispensable. After the eating and drinking, they spread out their blankets and have a snooze. In the afternoon there follow more bathing and more eating and drinking; and when there is a moon they stay late in order to enjoy it. Although everybody is dog tired, the return home is accompanied by laughter and singing.

EXERCISE 64

The Pilot Nagel

Nagel Harbor, Norwegian pilot at Colombo,—When he had given clear passage to the ships—Leaving for unknown and distant ports,—Would get down into his boat serious and thoughtful,—His thick arms crossed on his chest,—Smoking an old clay pipe.—And muttering slowly to himself in a northern tongue,—He would leave as soon as the ships vanished from sight.

Nagel Harbor, captain of cargo vessels,—Having travelled the world around, one day—got weary and stayed as a pilot in Colombo.—But he was always thinking of his far-off country—and the islands that are full of legend, the Lofoten.—But one day he died in the pilot-boat—Suddenly, after seeing off the tanker *Fjord Folden*,—As she steamed away·for the Lofoten Islands.

EXERCISE 65

Mike

They took Mike for a soldier.—He set out jauntily and happily—With Maris and Panayotis.—He couldn't even learn to slope arms—But kept muttering, Mr. Corporal,—Let me go back to my village.

Next year, in hospital,—He would stare speechless at the sky.—He fixed on some distant point—His meek nostalgic gaze,—As though he were saying, pleading,—Let me go to my home.

And Mike died a soldier.—He was seen off by some comrades,—Maris and Panayotis among them.—The hole was filled in above him,—But they left his foot sticking out.—He was a bit long, the poor chap.

EXERCISE 66

Alexandrian Kings

The Alexandrians gathered to see the children of Cleopatra —Caesarion and his younger brothers, Alexander and

Ptolemy—who for the first time were being brought out in the Gymnasium, there to be proclaimed kings amid the brilliant military parade.

Alexander they called King of Armenia, Media and the Parthians. Ptolemy they called King of Cilicia, Syria and Phoenicia. Caesarion stood in front of the others, dressed in rose-coloured silk, with a bunch of hyacinths at his breast, his belt a double row of sapphires and amethysts, his sandals tied with white ribbons with pink pearls embroidered on them. To him they gave a greater title than the younger ones: him they called the King of Kings.

The Alexandrians understood, of course, that all this was words and make-believe. But the day was warm and poetical, with the sky a pale blue; the Gymnasium of Alexandria was a triumphant masterpiece of art; the gorgeous dress of the courtiers something wonderful; and Caesarion was all charm and beauty (son of Cleopatra, blood of the Lagidae). So the Alexandrians came crowding to the festival, and they were enthusiastic and cheered in Greek and Egyptian (and some in Hebrew), delighted with the beautiful spectacle—though of course they knew what it was all really worth, what empty words those kingdoms were.

VOCABULARY

GREEK–ENGLISH

A

ἡ Ἀθήνα, Athens
ἀθόρυβα, noiselessly
τό Αἰγαῖο, Aegean
τό αἷμα, blood
ἀκόμα, still, yet, even
ἀκολουθῶ, I follow
ἀκούω, I hear (cf. *acou*stic)
ἀκριβής, exact
ἀκριβός, dear
ἡ Ἀκρόπολις, Acropolis
ἀλλά, but
ἀλλάζω, I change
ἀλλιῶς, otherwise
ἄλλος, other, different
ὁ ἄλλος, the other
ἄλλοτε, formerly
ἀλλοῦ, elsewhere
ἄλλωστε, besides
τό ἀμάξι, car, cab, cart
ἡ Ἀμερική, America
ἀμέσως, at once
ἡ ἀμμουδιά, sandy beach
ἀνάβω, I light
ἡ ἀνάγκη, need
ἡ Ἀνατολή, East
ἀνατολικά, to the east
ἀναφέρω, I mention
ἀνεβαίνω, I go up
ἀνήκω, I belong
ἀνήσυχος, uneasy
ὁ ἄνθρωπος, man, person
ἄνκαι, although, even if
ἀνόητος, silly
ἀνοιχτός, open
ἀντιλαμβάνομαι, I understand, perceive
ἀντίο, good-bye
ὁ ἄντρας, man, husband
ἡ ἀξία, value
ἀξίζει, it is worth
ὁ ἀξιωματικός, officer
ἀπαντῶ, I answer
ἀπαραίτητος, indispensable
ἀπέναντι, opposite
ἀπέχει, it is distant
ἀπίθανος, unlikely
ἁπλός, simple, plain
ἁπλώνω, I spread
ἀπό, from, by
τό ἀπόγευμα, afternoon
ἀπολαμβάνω, I enjoy
ἀπότομα, abruptly
ἀπόψε, tonight
ἀποφασίζω, I decide
ἡ ἀπόφασις, decision
ἀποφεύγω, I avoid
ἀποχτῶ, I get, acquire
ἀπροσδόκητα, unexpectedly
ἄραγε, (particle introducing question)
ἀργά, late, slowly
ἀριστερός, left
ἀρκετός, enough
τό ἀρνάκι, lamb
ἀρχίζω, I begin
τό ἀστεῖο, joke

ἀστεῖος, funny
τό ἀστέρι, star
ὁ ἀστυφύλακας, policeman
ἄσχημος, bad, ugly
ὁ Αὔγουστος, August
αὔριο, tomorrow
τό αὐτοκίνητο, motor-car
αὐτός, he, this
ἀφίνω, I let, leave
ἀφοῦ, since, after
ὁ Ἀχιλλεύς, Achilles

Β

βάζω, I put
βαθύς, deep
ἡ βάρκα, boat
βαρύς, heavy
τά βάσανα, troubles
ἡ βασιλεία, kingdom
ὁ βασιλιάς, king
βγαίνω, I go out
βέβαια, surely, of course
βέβαιος, sure
ἡ βεράντα, veranda
τό βιβλίο, book (cf. *Bible*)
ἡ βιβλιοθήκη, library
ὁ βλάκας, stupid person
τό βλέμμα, look
βλέπω, I see
ἡ βοήθεια, help, aid
βοηθῶ, I help
βολικός, convenient
βορινός, northern (cf. Aurora *Bor*ealis)
τό βουνό, mountain
βρίσκω, I find
βυθίζω, I sink, immerse

Γ

γαλάζιος, blue
ἡ Γαλλία, France (cf. *Gaul*)
γειά σου, your health! good-bye!
τό γέλιο, laughter
γελῶ, I laugh
γεμᾶτος, full
ἡ Γερμανία, Germany
γερός, strong and healthy
γιά, for, about
γιά νά, in order to
ὁ γιαλός, sea-shore
γιατί, why? because
γίνομαι, I become
τό γκαράζ, garage
τό γκαρσόν, waiter
γκρίζος, grey
γλυκύς, sweet (cf. *glu*cose)
ἡ γλῶσσα, tongue (cf. *gloss*ary)
γνωρίζω, I know (cf. a*gno*stic)
γοητευμένος, charmed
τό γράμμα, letter
τό γραμματόσημο, postage-stamp
τό γραφεῖο, office
γράφω, I write (cf. *graph*)
γρήγορος, quick
τά γυαλιά, spectacles
ὁ γυιός, son
τό γυμνάσιο, gymnasium, grammar school
ἡ γυναίκα, woman, wife (cf. *gynae*cologist)
γυρεύω, I look for
γυρίζω, I turn, return (cf. *gyro*)
ὁ γυρισμός, return
γύρω, round
ἡ γωνιά, corner (cf. tri*gono*metry)

Δ

τά δάκρυα, tears
δείχνω, I show, point at
δέκα, ten (cf. *dec*ade)
ὁ δεκανέας, corporal

δεκατρεῖς, thirteen
δεμένος, tied
δέν, negative particle
τό δέντρο, tree (cf. rhodo*dendron*)
δεξιά, to the right
ἡ Δευτέρα, Monday
δεύτερος, second (cf. *Deuter*-onomy)
διαβάζω, I read
ἡ διαδρομή, trip
διαθέσιμος, available
διακόσια, two hundred
τό διαμέρισμα, apartment, flat
διαπεραστικός, piercing
διαρκῶς, continually
διάφανος, transparent (cf. *dia-phanous*)
διάφοροι, different, various
ἡ διεύθυνσις, address
ὁ διευθυντής, director
δικός μου, mine
δίνω, I give
δίπλα, beside, next (to)
διπλός, double
δοκιμάζω, I try, sample
ἡ δουλειά, work
δουλεύω, I work
ἡ δραχμή, drachma
ὁ δρόμος, road, street, way (cf. *-drome*)
δροσερός, cool
δυνατός, strong (cf. *dyna*mic)
δύο, two
δυσκολεύομαι, I find it difficult
δύσκολος, difficult
δυστυχισμένος, unhappy
δώδεκα, twelve
τό δωμάτιο, room (cf. *dome*)

E

ὁ ἑαυτός μου, myself
ἡ ἑβδομάδα, week (cf. *hebdomad*al)
ἑβδομήντα, seventy
ἕβδομος, seventh
ἑβραΐκα, Hebrew
ἐγώ, I (cf. *ego*ist)
ἐδῶ, here
εἴκοσι, twenty
εἰκοστός, twentieth
εἰλικρινής, sincere
εἶμαι, I am
εἴτε . . . εἴτε, either . . . or
ἑκατό, a hundred (cf. *hecat*omb)
τό ἑκατομμύριο, million
ὁ ἑκατομμυριοῦχος, millionaire
ἑκατοστός, hundredth
ἡ ἐκδρομή, excursion, outing
ἐκεῖ, there
ἐκεῖνος, that, the other
ἡ ἔκπληξις, surprise
ἔκτακτος, excellent
ἕκτος, sixth
ἡ Ἑλλάδα, Greece (cf. *Hellas*)
ἑλληνικά, Greek
ἐμεῖς, we
ἡ ἐμορφιά, beauty
ἐμποδίζω, I prevent
ἐμπρός, in front
ἐμπροστά, in front
ἕνας, one, a
ἔνατος, ninth
ἐνενήντα, ninety
ἐνθουσιάζομαι, I get excited
ἐνιακόσια, nine hundred
ἐννιά, nine
ἕντεκα, eleven
ἐντελῶς, completely
ἐνῶ, while
ἑξακόσια, six hundred
ἐξαργυρώνω, I cash
ἐξετάζω, I examine
ἑξήντα, sixty
ἕξι, six

ἔξυπνος, intelligent, clever
ἔξω, out, outside (cf. *exotic*)
ἡ ἑορτή, holiday, festivity
ἐπευφημῶ, I cheer
τό ἐπίπεδο, level
ἑπόμενος, following
ἡ ἐποχή, season (cf. *epoch*)
ἐπ' ὤμου, slope arms
ὁ ἐργάτης, worker
τό ἔργο, work (artistic)
ἐρχόμενος, coming, next
ἡ ἐρώτησις, question
ἐσεῖς, you
τό ἑστιατόριο, restaurant
ἑτοιμάζομαι, I get ready
ἕτοιμος, ready
ἔτσι, so, thus
ἡ εὐγένεια, politeness
εὐγενής, polite, noble (cf. *eugen*ic)
εὔθυμος, merry, cheerful
εὔκολος, easy
εὐτυχής, happy
ἡ εὐτυχία, happiness
εὐτυχισμένος, happy
εὐχαριστημένος, pleased
εὐχάριστος, pleasant
εὐχαριστῶ, I thank (cf. *Eucharist*)
ἑφτά, seven
ἑφτακόσια, seven hundred
ἔχω, I have

Z

ζεστός, hot, warm (cf. *zest*)
τό ζευγάρι, couple, pair
τό ζήτημα, question, problem
ζητῶ, I ask for, look for
ἡ ζωή, life (cf. *zoo*logy)
ἡ ζώνη, belt (cf. *zone*)
ζῶ, I live

H

ἤ, or
ἡ ἡλιοθεραπεία, sunbathing
ὁ ἥλιος, sun (cf. *helio-*)
ἡ ἡσυχία, quiet
ἥσυχος, quiet

Θ

ἡ θάλασσα, sea
θαλασσινός, sea (adj.)
τό θάρρος, courage
θαρρῶ, I think
τό θαῦμα, miracle
θαυμάσιος, wonderful
τό θέαμα, spectacle
θεατρικός, theatrical
τό θέατρο, theatre
ἡ θεία, aunt
ὁ θεῖος, uncle
ἡ θέλησις, will
θέλω, I want
τό θέμα, subject (cf. *theme*)
οἱ Θερμοπύλες, Thermopylae
ἡ θέση, position, seat
ἡ Θεσσαλονίκη, Salonica
θριαμβικός, triumphal
ὁ θρύλος, legend
θυμᾶμαι, I remember
ὁ θυμός, anger
θυμώνω, I get angry, anger

I

ἰδιαίτερος, special
ἴδιος, same
ἡ ἰδιοτροπία, whim
ἰδιωτικός, private (cf. *idio*matic)
ἴσια, straight on
ἴσος, equal (cf. *iso*tope)
ἴσως, perhaps

ἡ ἱστορία, history, story
ἡ Ἰταλία, Italy

K

ἡ καθαριότης, cleanliness
καθαρός, clean (cf. *cathar*tic)
κάθε, every
τά καθέκαστα, particulars
καθιστός, sitting
κάθομαι, I sit
καθώς, as
καί, and, even
καινούριος, new
ὁ καιρός, weather, time
κακός, bad (cf. *caco*phony)
τό καλάθι, basket
καλημέρα, good morning
καληνύχτα, good night
ὁ καλλιτέχνης, artist
τό καλοκαίρι, summer
καλός, good, nice (cf. *calli*graphy)
καμαρωτός, jaunty
τό καμπαρέ, night-club
κάμποσος, a lot
κάν, at all
κανένας, no one, anyone
κανονίζω, I arrange (cf. *canon*)
κανονικός, regular
κάνω, I do, make
τό καπέλλο, hat
καπνίζω, I smoke
κάποιος, someone
κάποτε, sometime(s), then
τό καράβι, ship
ἡ καρδιά, heart (cf. *cardi*ac)
ἡ καρέκλα, chair
καρφώνω, I nail, fix
καταλαβαίνω, I understand
ὁ κατάλογος, list
κατάμαυρος, jet-black
καταπληκτικός, amazing
καταφέρνω, I succeed
κατεβαίνω, I go down
κάτι, something
κατοικῶ, I live
τό κατόρθωμα, feat
ἡ κατοχή, occupation
κάτω, down
τό καφενεῖο, café
ὁ καφές, coffee
κεντημένος, embroidered
τό κέντρο, centre, place of refreshment
τό κεφάλι, head (cf. *-cephalic*)
ὁ κῆπος, garden
κηρύττω, I proclaim, declare
κιόλας, already
κλαίω, I cry, weep
κλείω, I close
κοιμᾶμαι, I sleep
κοιτάζω, I look at
κολυμπῶ, I swim
τό κομμάτι, piece
ἡ κομψότητα, smartness
κοντά, near
ἡ κοπέλλα, girl
ἡ κορδέλλα, ribbon
τό κορίτσι, girl
ὁ κόσμος, world, people
ἡ κουβέντα, conversation
ἡ κουβέρτα, blanket
ἡ κουζίνα, kitchen
κουνῶ, I move
κουράζομαι, I get tired
ἡ κούραση, fatigue
κουρασμένος, tired
τό κουτί, box
κούφιος, empty, hollow
τό κρασί, wine
κρατημένος, reserved
ἡ κρεββατοκάμαρα, bedroom
τό κρίμα, pity

κρύβομαι, I hide
κρύος, cold
τό κρύσταλλο, ice, icicle, crystal
ἡ Κύπρος, Cyprus
κύρ, mister (familiar)
ἡ κυρία, Mrs., lady
ἡ Κυριακή, Sunday
ὁ κύριος, Mr., gentleman

Λ

ὁ λάκκος, hole, pit
λέγω, I say
λείπω, I am away, am lacking
ἡ λέξις, word (cf. *lex*icon)
τό λεπτό, minute
λεπτός, thin, delicate
ἡ Λευκωσία, Nicosia
τά λεφτά, money
τό λεωφορεῖο, bus
λησμονῶ, I forget
λίγο, a little
λίγος, a little, some
ὁ λιμένας, harbour
ἡ λίρα, pound sterling
ὁ λογαριασμός, bill
ὁ λόγος, speech, reason (cf. zoo*logy*)
τό Λονδίνο, London
λυπᾶμαι, I am sorry
λυπημένος, sad

M

μά, but
μαγευτικός, charming, delightful (cf. *mag*ic)
τό μαγιό, bathing costume
μαζεύω, I gather
μαζί, together
μαθαίνω, I learn (cf. poly*math*)
τό μάθημα, lesson
ὁ μαθητής, pupil
μακάρι, (particle introducing wish)
μακρινός, distant
μακριά, far
μακρύς, long
τά μαλλιά, hair
μᾶλλον, rather
ἡ μάννα, mother
τό μαργαριτάρι, pearl
τά μάτια, eyes
μαῦρος, black (cf. *Moor*)
τά μαχαιροπήρουνα, knives and forks
μέ, with
μεγάλος, big, great (cf. *mega-*)
μεθῶ, I get drunk (cf. *methyl*ated)
μένω, I stay
ἡ μέρα, day (cf. eph*emeral*)
ἡ μερίδα, portion
μερικοί, some
μέσα, in, inside
τό μεσημέρι, noon
τό μέσο, middle
μετά, after
τό μετάξι, silk
τό μῆλο, apple
μήπως, (particle introducing question)
ἡ μητέρα, mother
ἡ μηχανή, engine, machine
ἡ μηχανική, engineering
ὁ μηχανικός, engineer, mechanic
μιά, μία, one, a
μικρός, small (cf. *micro-*)
μιλῶ, I speak, talk
μισός, half
μοιάζω, I resemble
μόλις, as soon as, just
μολονότι, although

μόνο, only
μονολογῶ, I talk to myself
μόνος, alone, only
μονός, single
μουρμουρίζω, I murmur
ἡ μουσική, music
ἡ μπάλα, ball
τό μπάνιο, bath
τό μπάρ, bar
μπλέ, blue
μπορῶ, I can
τό μπουκάλι, bottle
τό μπράτσο, arm
μπροστά, in front
ἡ μπύρα, beer
τό μυαλό, brain
ἡ Μύκονος, Mykonos

N

νά (verbal particle)
ναί, yes
τά νέα, news
ἡ Νεάπολις, Naples
ὁ νεαρός, youth
ἡ Νέα Υόρκη, New York
νέος, young, new
τό νερό, water
τό νησί, island
νικῶ, I win, beat
νιώθω, I feel
τό νοίκι, rent
νομίζω, I think
ὁ Νορβηγός, Norwegian
τό νοσοκομεῖο, hospital
νοσταλγικός, nostalgic
ντρέπομαι, I am ashamed, I am shy
ντύνομαι, I get dressed
ἡ νύχτα, night
νωρίς, early

Ξ

ξαναβλέπω, I see again
ξαναδίνω, I give back, I give again
ξανθός, fair, blond
ξαπλώνω, I lie down
ξάφνου, suddenly
ξεκινῶ, I set off
τό ξενοδοχεῖο, hotel
ὁ ξένος, stranger, guest (cf. *xeno*phobia)
ξεπροβοδίζω, I see off
ξέρω, I know
ξεχνῶ, I forget
ξοδεύω, I spend
ξυπνῶ, I wake up

O

ὀγδόντα, eighty
ὄγδοος, eighth
ἡ ὁδός, street
ἡ οἰκογένεια, family
ὀκτακόσια, eight hundred
ὀκτώ, eight
ὁλάκερος, whole
ὅλο, all the time
ὁλόϊσια, straight on
ὁλόκληρος, whole
ὅλος, all
ὁλότελα, completely
ἡ ὁμιλία, talk (cf. *homily*)
ὅμως, but, nevertheless
τό ὄνομα, name
ὅποτε, whenever
ὅπου, where, wherever
ὅπως, as, like
ὁπωσδήποτε, in any case, without fail
ὄρθιος, standing
ὁ ὁρίζοντας, horizon

ορίστε, here you are
ἡ ὀροφή, roof
ὅσο, as much as
ὅτι, that
ὅ,τι, what
ὁ οὐρανός, sky (cf. *Uranus*)
οὔτε ... οὔτε, neither ... nor
ὄχι, no, not

Π

παγωμένος, frozen, ice-cold
τό παιδί, child (cf. *pedi*atry)
παίζω, I play
παίρνω, I take
τό παιχνίδι, game, toy
τό πακέτο, packet
πάλι, again
παλιός, old
τό παλτό, overcoat
ἡ Παναγία, Virgin Mary
τό Πανεπιστήμιο, University
πάντα, always
πάντοτε, always
παντρεύομαι, I marry
πάνω, up
πάρα πολύ, very much
ὁ παράδεισος, paradise
τό παράθυρο, window
παρακαλῶ, I request
παρακολουθῶ, I attend
παραξενεύομαι, I am taken aback
παράξενος, strange
ἡ Παρασκευή, Friday
ἡ παράταξη, parade
παρατῶ, I abandon
τό πάρτυ, party
ἡ πατάτα, potato
ὁ πατέρας, father
τό πάτωμα, floor
τό πεζοδρόμιο, pavement
πεθαίνω, I die
πειράζει, it matters
ἡ Πέμπτη, Thursday
πέμπτος, fifth
πενήντα, fifty
ἡ πέννα, pen, penny
πεντακόσια, five hundred
πέντε, five
πέρα, beyond
περίεργος, curious
περιμένω, I wait (for)
ἡ περιουσία, property
ἡ περιπέτεια, adventure
περιποιοῦμαι, I look after
περίπου, about
περισσότερος, more
περήφανος, proud
περίφημος, famous
περνῶ, I pass
περπατῶ, I walk
ἡ πετσέτα, towel, napkin
πέφτω, I fall
τό πεῦκο, pine-tree
πηγαίνω, I go
τό πιάνο, piano
πιάνω, I take hold of
τό πιάτο, plate
ἡ πιλοτίνα, pilot-boat
ὁ πιλότος, pilot
πίνω, I drink
πιό, more
πιότερο, more
τό πιοτό, drink
πιστεύω, I believe
πίσω, behind
πλάϊ, beside
πλατύς, wide (cf. *plat*ypus)
πληρέστατα, completely
ἡ πληροφορία, information
πληρώνω, I pay
πλησιάζω, I approach
ὁ πλοίαρχος, captain

τό πλοῖο, ship
πλούσιος, rich
ὁ πλοῦτος, wealth
πνευματικός, mental, spiritual
τό ποδάρι, foot
τά ποδήματα, shoes
τό πόδι, foot, leg
ποιητικός, poetic
ποιός; who?
ἡ ποιότητα, quality
ὁ πόλεμος, war (cf. *polemic*)
πολεμῶ, I fight
ἡ πόλις, city, town
πολλοί, many
ἡ πολυθρόνα, armchair
πολύς, much (cf. *poly-*)
ἡ πολυτέλεια, luxury
ἡ πορεία, course
ἡ πόρτα, door
πόσος; how much?
τό ποτάμι, river
πότε; when?
ποτέ, never, ever
τό ποτήρι, glass
ποῦ; where?
πού, that
τό πράγμα, thing (cf. *pragmatic*)
τό πρακτορεῖο, agency
πρᾶος, meek
πράσινος, green
πρέπει, it is necessary
πρίν, before
τίς προάλλες, the other day
τό πρόγευμα, breakfast
πρός, towards
προσέχω, I pay attention
προσκαλῶ, I invite
ἡ προσοχή, attention
προσπαθῶ, I try
τό πρόσωπο, face
ἡ πρόταση, suggestion, sentence
προτιμῶ, I prefer
προχωρῶ, I proceed
τό πρωϊνό, breakfast, morning
πρῶτος, first
πυκνός, thick
πῶς; how?
πώς, that

Ρ

τό ραδιόφωνο, radio
τά ρέστα, change
ἡ ρετσίνα, retsina (kind of wine)
ρίχνω, I throw
ροδόχρους, rose-coloured
τό ρολόϊ, clock, watch
ὁ Ρῶσσος, Russian
ρωτῶ, I ask, inquire

Σ

σά, like
τό Σάββατο, Saturday
ἡ σαλάτα, salad
τό σαλόνι, living room
ὁ σάπφειρος, sapphire
σαράντα, forty
σαχλός, inane, daft
σβύνω, I rub off
σέ, to
ἡ σειρά, row, series
τό σελίνι, shilling
σηκώνομαι, I get up
ἡ σημασία, meaning, importance (cf. *semantic*)
τό σημεῖο, point
σήμερα, today
σιγά, slowly
σιδηροδρομικῶς, by train
τό σινεμά, cinema
σιωπηλός, silent
ἡ σκάλα, staircase
σκεπάζω, I cover

σκέφτομαι, I think
ἡ σκέψη, thought
σκιερός, shady
σκληρός, cruel, hard
σκοπεύω, I intend
σοβαρός, serious
ὁ Σπαρτιάτης, Spartan
τό σπίρτο, match
τό σπίτι, house, home
σπουδαῖος, important
σταματῶ, I stop
τά σταφύλια, grapes
σταυρωμένος, crossed
στέκομαι, I stand
στέλλω, I send
στενοχωρημένος, worried
στεροῦμαι, I lack
τό στῆθος, breast
ἡ στιγμή, moment
στοιχίζω, I cost
ὁ στρατιώτης, soldier
στρίβω, I turn
τό στρίψιμο, turning
στρώνω, I spread
ὁ συγγραφέας, author
ἡ συγκέντρωση, meeting
συγκινημένος, moved
συγκινητικός, moving
συζητῶ, I discuss, argue
συλλογίζομαι, I ponder
συμφωνῶ, I agree
συναντιέμαι, I meet
ἡ συνέπεια, consequence
συνεπής, consistent
συνεχίζω, I continue
συνήθως, usually
συνοδεύω, I accompany
ὁ συνωστισμός, crowding
συχνά, often
συχνάζω, I frequent
σφίγγω, I squeeze
σχεδόν, almost
τό σχολεῖο, school
σωστός, correct, whole

T

ἡ ταβέρνα, tavern, pub
ἡ τάξη, class
τό ταξί, taxi
τό ταξίδι, journey
τέλειος, perfect
τελειώνω, I finish
τελείως, completely
τελευταῖος, last
τό τέλος, end
τέσσερεις, four
ἡ Τετάρτη, Wednesday
τό τέταρτο, quarter
τέταρτος, fourth
τετρακόσιοι, four hundred
ἡ τέχνη, art (cf. *tech*nique)
τό τζάκι, hearth, fireplace
ἡ τηλεόρασις, television
τό τηλέφωνο, telephone
τηλεφωνῶ, I telephone
τί; what?
τινάζω, I push away
τίποτε, nothing, anything
τονίζω, I stress (cf. *tone*)
τόσο, so
τότε, then
τουριστικός, tourist (adj.)
τό τραγούδι, song
τραγουδῶ, I sing
τό τραίνο, train
ἡ τράπεζα, bank
τό τραπεζάκι, small table
τό τραπέζι, table
τρεῖς, three
τρέχω, I run
τριακόσιοι, three hundred
τριάντα, thirty
τριανταφυλλίς, rose-coloured

ἡ *Τρίτη*, Tuesday
τρίτος, third
τό *τρόλλεϋ*, trolley-bus
τρομάζω, I get frightened
τρομερά, awfully
τρώγω, I eat
τό *τσάϊ*, tea
ἡ *τσάντα*, handbag
τό *τσιγάρο*, cigarette
τό *τσιμπούκι*, pipe
τυχερός, lucky
τώρα, now

Υ

ὁ *ὑάκινθος*, hyacinth
ὑπέροχος, excellent
ὁ *ὕπνος*, sleep
ἡ *ὑπόθεσις*, case, matter
ὑπόσχομαι, I promise
ὑπόχρεος, obliged
ὑποχρεωμένος, forced
ὕστερα, after

Φ

τό *φαγητό*, food, meal
τό *φαγοπότι*, eating and drinking
τό *φαΐ*, food, meal
φαίνομαι, appear, seem
ὁ *φαντάρος*, soldier
τό *φεγγάρι*, moon
φέρω, I bring
φεύγω, I go away
τό *φθινόπωρο*, autumn
τό *φίλμ*, film
ὁ *φίλος*, friend (cf. *phil-*)
ὁ *φιλόσοφος*, philosopher
τό *φλυντζάνι*, cup
φοβᾶμαι, I am afraid
ἡ *φορά*, time
φορτηγός, cargo (adj.)
ὁ *φουκαράκος*, poor chap
ὁ *φοῦρνος*, oven, furnace
φροντίζω, I take care
τό *φροῦτο*, fruit
φτάνω, I reach
φτωχός, poor
φυσικά, naturally
φυσῶ, I blow
φωνάζω, I cry
ἡ *φωνή*, voice (cf. *phon*etic)
τό *φῶς*, light
ἡ *φωτιά*, fire
φωτισμένος, lighted
ἡ *φωτογραφία*, photograph

Χ

χαϊδεμένος, pampered
χαϊδεύω, pamper, caress
ὁ *χαιρετισμός*, greeting
χαίρομαι, I am glad
χαλῶ, I spoil, demolish, change
χαμένος, lost
χαμηλός, low
τό *χαμόγελο*, smile
χαμογελῶ, I smile
χάμω, on the ground
χάνω, I lose
ἡ *χαρά*, joy
ἡ *χάρη*, grace, charm
χαρούμενος, joyful
τό *χαρτί*, paper
τά *χαρτιά*, cards
χάρτινος, paper (adj.)
τό *χαρτονόμισμα*, currency note
τά *χείλη*, lips
χειρότερος, worse
τό *χέρι*, hand, arm
χθές, yesterday

χίλια, a thousand
χοντρός, fat, thick
χορεύω, I dance
ὁ χορός, dance, chorus
τά χρήματα, money
χρήσιμος, useful
ὁ χρόνος, year, time (cf. *chronology*)
χρυσός, gold
τό χρῶμα, colour (cf. *chrome*)
χρωστῶ, I owe
χωμάτινος, earthen
ἡ χώρα, country
τό χωριό, village
χωρίς, without

Ψ

ψάχνω, I search
τό ψέμα, lie (cf. *pseudo-*)
ψηλός, tall
ψητός, baked, roast
ψόφιος, lifeless
ψυχρός, cold

Ω

ἡ ὥρα, hour, time
ὡραῖος, beautiful
ὥς, till, up to
ὥσπου, till
ὥστε, so that

ENGLISH-GREEK

A

a, an, ἕνας
I abandon, παρατῶ
about, γιά, περίπου
abruptly, ἀπότομα
I accompany, συνοδεύω
I acquire, ἀποκτῶ
address, ἡ διεύθυνσις
adventure, ἡ περιπέτεια
afraid, I am, φοβᾶμαι
after, μετά, ὕστερα
afternoon, τό ἀπόγευμα
again, πάλι, ξανά
agency, τό πρακτορεῖο
I agree, συμφωνῶ
aid, ἡ βοήθεια
all, ὅλος
almost, σχεδόν
alone, μόνος
already, κιόλας
although, ἄν καί, μολονότι
always, πάντα, πάντοτε
I am, εἶμαι
amazing, καταπληκτικός
and, καί
anger, ὁ θυμός
I answer, ἀπαντῶ
anyone, κάποιος, κανένας
anything, κάτι, τίποτε
apartment, τό διαμέρισμα
I appear, φαίνομαι
apple, τό μῆλο
I approach, πλησιάζω
I argue, συζητῶ
arm, τό μπράτσο, τό χέρι
armchair, ἡ πολυθρόνα
art, ἡ τέχνη
artist, ὁ καλλιτέχνης
as, καθώς, ὅπως
as much as, ὅσο
as soon as, μόλις
ashamed, I am, ντρέπομαι
I ask, ρωτῶ
I ask for, ζητῶ
at once, ἀμέσως
Athens, ἡ Ἀθήνα
I attend, παρακολουθῶ
attention, ἡ προσοχή
aunt, ἡ θεία
author, ὁ συγγραφέας
autumn, τό φθινόπωρο
available, διαθέσιμος
I avoid, ἀποφεύγω
away, I am, λείπω
awfully, τρομερά

B

bad, κακός, ἄσχημος
ball, ἡ μπάλα
bank, ἡ τράπεζα
bar, τό μπάρ
basket, τό καλάθι
bath, τό μπάνιο
bathing costume, τό μαγιό
beautiful, ὡραῖος
beauty, ἡ ἐμορφιά
because, γιατί
I become, γίνομαι
bedroom, ἡ κρεββατοκάμαρα
beer, ἡ μπύρα
before, πρίν
I begin, ἀρχίζω

behind, *πίσω*
I believe, *πιστεύω*
I belong, *ἀνήκω*
belt, *ἡ ζώνη*
beside, *δίπλα, πλάϊ*
besides, *ἄλλωστε*
beyond, *πέρα*
big, *μεγάλος*
bill, *ὁ λογαριασμός*
black, *μαῦρος*
blanket, *ἡ κουβέρτα*
blond, *ξανθός*
blood, *τό αἷμα*
I blow, *φυσῶ*
blue, *γαλάζιος, μπλέ*
boat, *ἡ βάρκα*
book, *τό βιβλίο*
bottle, *τό μπουκάλι*
box, *τό κουτί*
brain, *τό μυαλό*
breakfast, *τό πρόγευμα, τό πρωϊνό*
breast, *τό στῆθος*
I bring, *φέρω*
bus, *τό λεωφορεῖο*
but, *ἀλλά, μά, ὅμως*
by, *κοντά, μέ*
by train, *σιδηροδρομικῶς*

C

café, *τό καφενεῖο*
I can, *μπορῶ*
captain, *ὁ πλοίαρχος*
car, *τό αὐτοκίνητο, τό ἁμάξι*
cards, *τά χαρτιά*
I caress, *χαϊδεύω*
I cash, *ἐξαργυρώνω*
centre, *τό κέντρο*
cheerful, *εὔθυμος*
chair, *ἡ καρέκλα*
I change, *ἀλλάζω, χαλῶ*
change, *τά ρέστα*
charm, *ἡ χάρη*
charmed, *γοητευμένος*
charming, *μαγευτικός*
child, *τό παιδί*
cigarette, *τό τσιγάρο*
cinema, *τό σινεμά*
city, *ἡ πόλις*
class, *ἡ τάξη*
clean, *καθαρός*
cleanliness, *ἡ καθαριότης*
clever, *ἔξυπνος*
clock, *τό ρολόϊ*
I close, *κλείω*
coffee, *ὁ καφές*
cold, *κρύος, ψυχρός*
colour, *τό χρῶμα*
completely, *ἐντελῶς*
consequence, *ἡ συνέπεια*
consistent, *συνεπής*
I continue, *συνεχίζω*
continually, *διαρκῶς*
convenient, *βολικός*
conversation, *ἡ κουβέντα*
cool, *δροσερός*
corner, *ἡ γωνιά*
corporal, *ὁ δεκανέας*
correct, *σωστός*
I cost, *στοιχίζω*
country, *ἡ χώρα*
couple, *τό ζευγάρι*
courage, *τό θάρρος*
course, *ἡ πορεία*
I cover, *σκεπάζω*
crowding, *ὁ συνωστισμός*
cruel, *σκληρός*
I cry, *κλαίω, φωνάζω*
crystal, *τό κρύσταλλο*
cup, *τό φλυντζάνι*
curious, *περίεργος*
currency note, *τό χαρτονόμισμα*
Cyprus, *ἡ Κύπρος*

D

dance, ὁ χορός
I dance, χορεύω
day, ἡ μέρα
dear, ἀκριβός
I decide, ἀποφασίζω
decision, ἡ ἀπόφασις
deep, βαθύς
delicate, λεπτός
I demolish, χαλῶ
I die, πεθαίνω
different, διάφορος
difficult, δύσκολος
director, ὁ διευθυντής
I discuss, συζητῶ
distant, μακρινός
distant, it is, ἀπέχει
I do, κάνω
door, ἡ πόρτα
double, διπλός
down, κάτω
I drink, πίνω

E

early, νωρίς
east, ἡ ἀνατολή
easy, εὔκολος
I eat, τρώγω
eight, ὀκτώ
eight hundred, ὀκτακόσια
eighty, ὀγδόντα
either ... or, εἴτε ... εἴτε
eleven, ἕντεκα
elsewhere, ἀλλοῦ
end, τό τέλος
engine, ἡ μηχανή
engineer, ὁ μηχανικός
engineering, ἡ μηχανική
I enjoy, ἀπολαμβάνω
enough, ἀρκετός
equal, ἴσος
even, ἀκόμα
even if, ἄνκαι
ever, ποτέ
every, κάθε
eyes, τά μάτια
exact, ἀκριβής
I examine, ἐξετάζω
excellent, ἔκτακτος, ὑπέροχος
excursion, ἡ ἐκδρομή

F

face, τό πρόσωπο
fair, ξανθός
I fall, πέφτω
family, ἡ οἰκογένεια
famous, περίφημος
far, μακριά
fat, χοντρός
father, ὁ πατέρας
fatigue, ἡ κούραση
feat, τό κατόρθωμα
I feel, νιώθω
fifty, πενήντα
I fight, πολεμῶ
film, τό φίλμ
I finish, τελειώνω
I find, βρίσκω
I find it difficult, δυσκολεύομαι
fire, ἡ φωτιά
first, πρῶτος
five, πέντε
five hundred, πεντακόσια
flat, τό διαμέρισμα
floor, τό πάτωμα
follow, ἀκολουθῶ
following, ἑπόμενος
food, τό φαγητό, τό φαΐ
foot, τό πόδι
for, γιά
forced, ὑποχρεωμένος

I forget, λησμονῶ, ξεχνῶ
formerly, ἄλλοτε
forty, σαράντα
four, τέσσερεις
four hundred, τετρακόσιοι
France, ἡ Γαλλία
I frequent, συχνάζω
Friday, ἡ Παρασκευή
friend, ὁ φίλος
from, ἀπό
frozen, παγωμένος
fruit, τό φροῦτο
full, γεμᾶτος
funny, ἀστεῖος
furnace, ὁ φοῦρνος

G

game, τό παιχνίδι
garage, τό γκαράζ
garden, ὁ κῆπος
I gather, μαζεύω
gentleman, ὁ κύριος
Germany, ἡ Γερμανία
I get angry, θυμώνω
I get dressed, ντύνομαι
I get frightened, τρομάζω
I get ready, ἑτοιμάζομαι
I get tired, κουράζομαι
I get up, σηκώνομαι
girl, τό κορίτσι, ἡ κοπέλλα
I give, δίνω
glad, I am, χαίρομαι
glass, τό ποτήρι
I go, πηγαίνω
I go away, φεύγω
I go down, κατεβαίνω
I go out, βγαίνω
I go up, ἀνεβαίνω
gold, ὁ χρυσός
good, καλός
good-bye, ἀντίο, γειά σου
good morning, καλημέρα
good night, καληνύχτα
grace, ἡ χάρη
grammar-school, τό γυμνάσιο
grapes, τά σταφύλια
great, μεγάλος
Greece, ἡ Ἑλλάδα
Greek, ἑλληνικός
green, πράσινος
greeting, ὁ χαιρετισμός
grey, γκρίζος
guest, ὁ ξένος

H

hair, τά μαλλιά
half, μισός
hand, τό χέρι
handbag, ἡ τσάντα
happiness, ἡ εὐτυχία
happy, εὐτυχής, εὐτυχισμένος
harbour, τό λιμάνι
hard, σκληρός
hat, τό καπέλλο
I have, ἔχω
he, αὐτός
head, τό κεφάλι
I hear, ἀκούω
heart, ἡ καρδιά
heavy, βαρύς
help, ἡ βοήθεια
I help, βοηθῶ
here, ἐδῶ
I hide, κρύβω, κρύβομαι
history, ἡ ἱστορία
holiday, ἡ ἑορτή
home, τό σπίτι
horizon, ὁ ὁρίζοντας
hospital, τό νοσοκομεῖο
hot, ζεστός
hotel, τό ξενοδοχεῖο
hour, ἡ ὥρα

house, τό σπίτι
how, πῶς
how much, πόσος
a hundred, ἑκατό
husband, ὁ ἄντρας

I

I, ἐγώ
I immerse, βυθίζω
important, σπουδαῖος
in, μέσα
in front, μπροστά
in order to, γιά νά
indispensable, ἀπαραίτητος
information, ἡ πληροφορία
I inquire, ρωτῶ
inside, μέσα
intelligent, ἔξυπνος
I intend, σκοπεύω
I invite, προσκαλῶ
island, τό νησί, ἡ νῆσος
Italy, ἡ 'Ιταλία

J

joke, τό ἀστεῖο
journey, τό ταξίδι
joy, ἡ χαρά

K

king, ὁ βασιλιάς
kitchen, ἡ κουζίνα
I know, ξέρω, γνωρίζω

L

I lack, στεροῦμαι
lady, ἡ κυρία
lamb, τό ἀρνάκι
last, τελευταῖος
late, ἀργά
I laugh, γελῶ
laughter, τό γέλιο
I learn, μαθαίνω
left, ἀριστερός
legend, ὁ θρύλος
lesson, τό μάθημα
I let, ἀφίνω
letter, τό γράμμα
level, τό ἐπίπεδο
library, ἡ βιβλιοθήκη
lie, τό ψέμα
I lie down, ξαπλώνω
life, ἡ ζωή
lifeless, ψόφιος
light, τό φῶς
I light, ἀνάβω
lighted, φωτισμένος
like, σά
lips, τά χείλη
list, ὁ κατάλογος
little, λίγος, μικρός
I live, ζῶ
living room, τό σαλόνι
London, τό Λονδίνο
long, μακρύς
look, τό βλέμμα
I look at, κοιτάζω
I look for, γυρεύω, ζητῶ
I lose, χάνω
lost, χαμένος
a lot, κάμποσος
low, χαμηλός
lucky, τυχερός

M

machine, ἡ μηχανή
I make, κάνω
man, ὁ ἄνθρωπος, ὁ ἄντρας
many, πολλοί
I marry, παντρεύομαι

match, τό σπίρτο
it matters, πειράζει
meal, τό φαγητό
meaning, ἡ σημασία
mechanic, ὁ μηχανικός
I meet, συναντῶ
meeting, ἡ συγκέντρωση
mental, πνευματικός
I mention, ἀναφέρω
merry, εὔθυμος
middle, μέσος
million, τό ἑκατομμύριο
millionaire, ὁ ἑκατομμυριοῦχος
mine, δικός μου
minute, τό λεπτό
miracle, τό θαῦμα
Mr., ὁ κύριος
Mrs., ἡ κυρία
moment, ἡ στιγμή
Monday, ἡ Δευτέρα
money, τά λεφτά, τά χρήματα
moon, τό φεγγάρι
more, περισσότερος
more (*adv.*), πιό
morning, τό πρωί, τό πρωινό
mother, ἡ μητέρα, ἡ μάννα
motor-car, τό αὐτοκίνητο
mountain, τό βουνό
I move, κουνῶ
moving, συγκινητικός
much, πολύς
I murmur, μουρμουρίζω
music, ἡ μουσική

N

name, τό ὄνομα
napkin, ἡ πετσέτα
naturally, φυσικά
near, κοντά
necessary, it is, πρέπει
need, ἡ ἀνάγκη
neither . . . nor, οὔτε . . . οὔτε
never, ποτέ
nevertheless, ὅμως
new, νέος, καινούριος
news, τά νέα
next, ἑπόμενος, ἐρχόμενος
nice, καλός, ὡραῖος
Nicosia, ἡ Λευκοσία
night, ἡ νύχτα
night-club, τό καμπαρέ
nine, ἐννιά
nine hundred, ἐννιακόσιοι
ninety, ἐνενήντα
no, ὄχι
no one, κανένας
noiselessly, ἀθόρυβα
noon, τό μεσημέρι
northern, βόρειος, βορινός
nothing, τίποτε

O

obliged, ὑπόχρεος
of course, βέβαια, βεβαίως
office, τό γραφεῖο
officer, ὁ ἀξιωματικός
often, συχνά
old, παλιός
one, ἕνας
only, μόνο
open, ἀνοιχτός
opposite, ἀπέναντι
or, ἤ
other, ἄλλος
otherwise, ἀλλιῶς
out, ἔξω
outing, ἡ ἐκδρομή
outside, ἔξω
oven, ὁ φοῦρνος
overcoat, τό παλτό
I owe, χρωστῶ

P

packet, τό πακέτο
pair, τό ζευγάρι
paper, τό χαρτί
parade, ἡ παράταξη
paradise, ὁ παράδεισος
party, τό πάρτυ
I pass, περνῶ
pavement, τό πεζοδρόμιο
I pay, πληρώνω
I pay attention, προσέχω
pearl, τό μαργαριτάρι
pen, ἡ πέννα
penny, ἡ πέννα
people, ὁ κόσμος
perfect, τέλειος
philosopher, ὁ φιλόσοφος
photograph, ἡ φωτογραφία
piano, τό πιάνο
piercing, διαπεραστικός
pilot, ὁ πιλότος
pine-tree, τό πεῦκο
pity, τό κρίμα
plate, τό πιάτο
I play, παίζω
pleasant, εὐχάριστος
pleased, εὐχαριστημένος
piece, τό κομμάτι
poetic, ποιητικός
point, τό σημεῖο
I point at, δείχνω
policeman, ὁ ἀστυφύλακας
polite, εὐγενής
politeness, ἡ εὐγένεια
poor, φτωχός
portion, ἡ μερίδα
position, ἡ θέση
postage-stamp, τό γραμματόσημο
potato, ἡ πατάτα
pound (sterling), ἡ λίρα
I prefer, προτιμῶ
I prevent, ἐμποδίζω
private, ἰδιωτικός
problem, τό πρόβλημα, τό ζήτημα
I proceed, προχωρῶ
I promise, ὑπόσχομαι
property, ἡ περιουσία
proud, περήφανος
pub, ἡ ταβέρνα
pupil, ὁ μαθητής
I put, βάζω

Q

quality, ἡ ποιότητα
quarter, τό τέταρτο
question, ἡ ἐρώτησις
quick, γρήγορος
quiet, ἥσυχος
quietness, ἡ ἡσυχία

R

radio, τό ραδιόφωνο
rather, μᾶλλον
I reach, φτάνω
I read, διαβάζω
ready, ἕτοιμος
reason, ὁ λόγος
regular, κανονικός
I remember, θυμᾶμαι
rent, τό νοίκι
I request, παρακαλῶ
I resemble, μοιάζω
reserved, κρατημένος
restaurant, τό ἑστιατόριο
I return, γυρίζω
ribbon, κορδέλλα
rich, πλούσιος
river, τό ποτάμι
road, ὁ δρόμος

roast, ψητός
roof, ἡ ὀροφή
room, τό δωμάτιο
round, γύρω
row, σειρά
I rub off, σβύνω
I run, τρέχω

S

sad, λυπημένος
salad, ἡ σαλάτα
Salonica, ἡ Θεσσαλονίκη
same, ἴδιος
Saturday, τό Σάββατο
I say, λέγω
sea, ἡ θάλασσα, ὁ γιαλός
I search, ψάχνω
season, ἡ ἐποχή
second, δεύτερος
I see, βλέπω
I seem, φαίνομαι
I send, στέλλω
sentence, ἡ πρόταση
series, ἡ σειρά
serious, σοβαρός
I set off, ξεκινῶ
seven, ἑπτά
seven hundred, ἑφτακόσια
seventy, ἑβδομήντα
shady, σκιερός
shilling, τό σελίνι
ship, τό πλοῖο, τό καράβι
shoes, τά παπούτσια
I show, δείχνω
silent, σιωπηλός
silk, τό μετάξι
silly, ἀνόητος
simple, ἁπλός
since, ἀφοῦ
sincere, εἰλικρινής
I sing, τραγουδῶ
single, μονός
I sit, κάθομαι
six, ἕξι
six hundred, ἑξακόσιοι
sixty, ἑξήντα
sky, ὁ οὐρανός
sleep, ὁ ὕπνος
I sleep, κοιμᾶμαι
slowly, σιγά, ἀργά
small, μικρός
smartness, ἡ κομψότητα
smile, τό χαμόγελο
I smile, χαμογελῶ
I smoke, καπνίζω
so, ἔτσι, τόσο
soldier, ὁ στρατιώτης
some, λίγος, μερικοί
someone, κάποιος
something, κάτι
sometime(s), κάποτε
son, ὁ γυιός
song, τό τραγούδι
sorry, I am, λυπᾶμαι
I speak, μιλῶ
special, ἰδιαίτερος
spectacle, τό θέαμα
spectacles, τά γυαλιά
speech, ὁ λόγος
I spend, ξοδεύω
I spoil, χαλῶ
I spread, ἁπλώνω
staircase, ἡ σκάλα
I stand, στέκομαι
standing, ὄρθιος
star, τό ἄστρο, τό ἀστέρι
I stay, μένω
still, ἀκόμα
I stop, σταματῶ
story, ἡ ἱστορία
straight on, ἴσια
strange, παράξενος
stranger, ὁ ξένος

street, ὁδρόμος, ἡ ὁδός
I stress, τονίζω
strong, δυνατός
stupid person, ὁ βλάκας
subject, τό θέμα
suddenly, ξαφνικά
summer, τό καλοκαίρι
sun, ὁ ἥλιος
sunbathing, ἡ ἡλιοθεραπεία
Sunday, ἡ Κυριακή
sure, βέβαιος
surely, βέβαια
surprise, ἡ ἔκπληξη
sweet, γλυκύς, γλυκός
I swim, κολυμπῶ

T

table, τό τραπέζι
I take, παίρνω
I take care, φροντίζω
I take hold of, πιάνω
talk, ἡ ὁμιλία
I talk, μιλῶ
tall, ψηλός
taxi, τό ταξί
tea, τό τσάϊ
tears, τά δάκρυα
telephone, τό τηλέφωνο
I telephone, τηλεφωνῶ
television, ἡ τηλεόρασις
ten, δέκα
I thank, εὐχαριστῶ
that, ἐκεῖνος, ὅτι, πώς
theatre, τό θέατρο
then, τότε
thick, πυκνός
thin, λεπτός
thing, τό πράγμα
I think, νομίζω, θαρρῶ, σκέφτομαι
thirteen, δεκατρεῖς
thirty, τριάντα
this, αὐτός
thought, ἡ σκέψη
a thousand, χίλιοι
three, τρεῖς
three hundred, τριακόσιοι
I throw, ρίχνω
Thursday, ἡ Πέμπτη
thus, ἔτσι
tied, δεμένος
till, ὥς, ὥσπου
time, ὁ χρόνος, ἡ ὥρα
tired, κουρασμένος
to, σέ
today, σήμερα
together, μαζί
tomorrow, αὔριο
tongue, ἡ γλῶσσα
tonight, ἀπόψε
towards, πρός
town, ἡ πόλις
train, τό τραίνο
tree, τό δέντρο
troubles, τά βάσανα
I try, δοκιμάζω, προσπαθῶ
I turn, γυρίζω, στρίβω
turning, τό στρίψιμο
twelve, δώδεκα
twenty, εἴκοσι
two, δύο
two hundred, διακόσιοι

U

ugly, ἄσχημος
uncle, ὁ θεῖος
I understand, καταλαβαίνω, ἀντιλαμβάνομαι
uneasy, ἀνήσυχος
unexpectedly, ἀπροσδόκητα
unhappy, δυστυχισμένος
University, τό Πανεπιστήμιο

unlikely, ἀπίθανος
up, πάνω
up to, ὥς
useful, χρήσιμος
usually, συνήθως

V

value, ἡ ἀξία
various, διάφοροι
veranda, ἡ βεράντα
very much, πάρα πολύ
village, τό χωριό
Virgin Mary, ἡ Παναγία
voice, ἡ φωνή

W

I wait, περιμένω
waiter, τό γκαρσόν
I wake up, ξυπνῶ
I walk, περπατῶ
I want, θέλω
war, ὁ πόλεμος
warm, ζεστός
watch, τό ρολόϊ
water, τό νερό
way, ὁ δρόμος
we, ἐμεῖς
wealth, ὁ πλοῦτος
weather, ὁ καιρός
Wednesday, ἡ Τετάρτη
week, ἡ ἑβδομάδα
I weep, κλαίω
what? τί; ὅ,τι
when? πότε;
whenever, ὅποτε
where? ποῦ;
where, ὅπου
while, ἐνῶ
whim, ἡ ἰδιοτροπία
who? ποιός;
whole, ὁλάκερος, ὁλόκληρος, σωστός
why? γιατί;
wide, πλατύς
wife, ἡ γυναίκα
will, ἡ θέλησις
I win, νικῶ
window, τό παράθυρο
wine, τό κρασί
with, μέ
without, χωρίς
without fail, ὁπωσδήποτε
woman, ἡ γυναῖκα
wonderful, θαυμάσιος
word, ἡ λέξις
work, ἡ δουλειά
I work, δουλεύω
worker, ὁ ἐργάτης
world, ὁ κόσμος
worried, στενοχωρημένος
worse, χειρότερος
worth, it is, ἀξίζει
I write, γράφω

Y

year, ὁ χρόνος
yes, ναί
yesterday, χθές
yet, ἀκόμα
you, ἐσεῖς
young, νέος
youth, νέος, νεαρός

NEW TESTAMENT GREEK

D. F. HUDSON

A practical and lively introduction to Koine, the popular Greek language of the First Century AD in which the New Testament was written.

This book is divided into a series of graded lessons and exercises in which the student is progressively introduced to the grammar, vocabulary and sentence structures of the language. It is designed both for the ordinary reader and the theology student as an invaluable and enjoyable aid to a deeper understanding of the Scriptures.

TEACH YOURSELF BOOKS

ANCIENT GREEK
A Complete Course

GAVIN BETTS and ALAN HENRY

An introduction to the language of the people who began Western civilisation.

This book presents the Ancient Greek language clearly and precisely, without academic stuffiness or unnecessary detail. Each of the 25 units contains grammar practice and a reading exercise, with a revision section provided at the end of the book. Additional information on topics such as the history of the Greek language is included to broaden the reader's interest.

Apart from Unit 2, all sentences and passages in the reading exercises are original Greek with changes kept to an absolute minimum.

TEACH YOURSELF BOOKS